A CREATE AND UPDATE

AN UNRESOURCED PROJECT

USING

ELECOSOFT (ASTA) POWERPROJECT

VERSION 15.2

BY

PAUL EASTWOOD HARRIS

2-day training course

handout and student workshops

© *Eastwood Harris Pty Ltd*

ASTA NAME CHANGE

Asta plc was purchased by Elecosoft plc and the term Asta has been dropped in all text published by Elecosoft plc in Powerproject Version 15. Many people and most overseas authorised distributor websites at the time of publishing this book refer to Powerproject as "Asta" so as a result I have named this book with the term "Asta".

DISCLAIMER

The information contained in this book is, to the best of the author's knowledge, true and correct. The author has made every effort to ensure accuracy of this publication but cannot be held responsible for any loss or damage arising from any information in this book.

AUTHOR AND PUBLISHER

Paul E Harris
Eastwood Harris Pty Ltd
PO Box 4032
Doncaster Heights 3109
Victoria
Australia
harrispe@eh.com.au
http://www.eh.com.au
Tel: +61 (0)4 1118 7701

28 August 2020

ISBN 978-1-925185-75-1 (1-925185-75-3)

Workshop 1 – Creating a Project

Notes on Date Format

The date format displayed in Asta dialogue boxes, such as the **Start Date** in the **File**, **New** form, is adopted from your **System Short Date** format. You may change your **System Short Date** from **Start**, **Settings**, **Time and Language** in earlier Windows operating systems and in later Windows operating systems in **Settings**, **Region**, **Change date, time or number formats**. This change will also change the date format in many apps such as **File Explorer** and **Outlook**.

The workshops text displays the format of dd-MMM-yy and display dates as 06-Dec-21.

Note: There are some slides with the date format of dd-mm-yy, 06-12-21.

Background

You are an employee of OzBuild Ltd and are responsible for planning the bid preparation required to ensure that a response to an RFQ (Request For Quote) for Wilson International is submitted on time.

Your company has completed the Start-up Phase of the project, the Bid Strategy has been developed and approval to bid for this project has been given.

You have been requested to plan the project Bid Phase, where the Bid will be produced, which comprises of the following deliverables/products:

- Technical Specification
- Delivery Plan
- Bid Document.

You have been advised that the RFQ will not be available until the 06 December 2021.

These workshops will take you through the process of creating the Initiating Phase Plan for the development of the Bid to be submitted in response to the RFQ.

 A project template in *.pp format titled "Australian and US Version 15 Asta Powerproject construction template" has been loaded on the Eastwood Harris web site at www.eh.com.au **Software Downloads** page that has a number of the issues with trying to use the UK templates in the US or Australia resolved, including the default currency has been set to $'s and calendar holidays revised. You should download this file, open it and save it as a template and use this file instead of the Asta supplied UK templates.

If you do not use this template you will receive different results.

If you use a different currency then you may create your countries currency and assign it and still use this template.

Assignment

1. Download Asta Powerproject template "Australian and US Asta Version 15 Powerproject construction template" has been loaded on the Eastwood Harris web site at www.eh.com.au Software Downloads page, or use a template supplied by your trainer.

2. Open it and save in the Asta Templates directory or drag this template in the Documents/Asta Powerproject/Templates subdirectory:

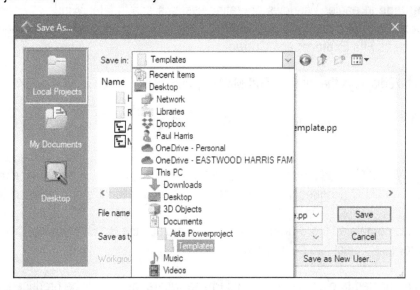

3. Close all projects.
4. Create a new project by selecting **File**, **New** and select an appropriate template,
5. Create your project with the file name of **OzBuild** in a location of your choice, such as the desktop,
6. Title – **OzBuild Bid**,
7. For – **Wilson International**,
8. By – enter your name,
9. Set the **Start date:** to **Mon 06 Dec 21**,
10. Press the **Create** button to save the data.

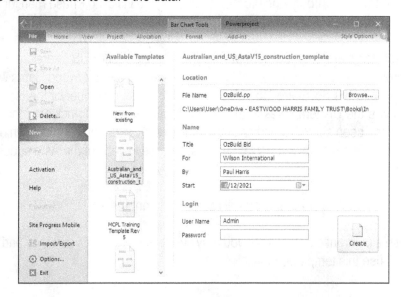

11. Check the currency unit of Dollar exists by selecting **View**, **Show**, **Library Explorer**:

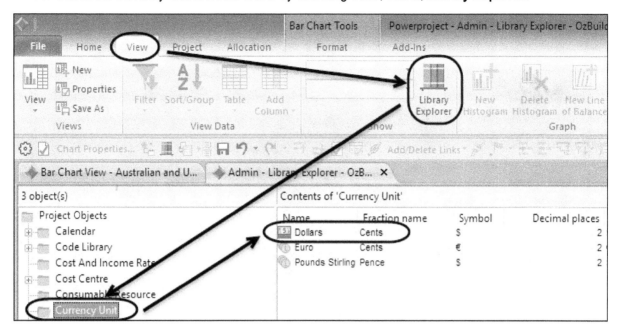

12. An additional window and tab is now open, you may close this by clicking on the **X**:

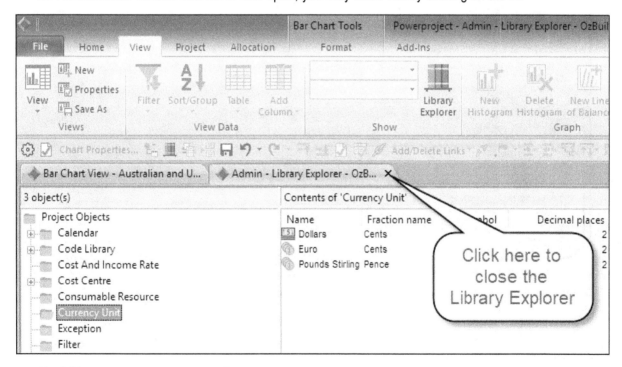

13. Add your countries currency if it does not exist.

14. Select **File**, **Options**, **View** tab and check that your countries currency is set as the Default Currency.

15. If you wish to change the currency to your country's currency, then do that now from the drop down box.

NOTE: Completed workshops and PowerPoint Instructors slide presentations may be downloaded from the Eastwood Harris web site at www.eh.com.au.

Workshop 2 – Navigation and Setting Options

Background
In this workshop you will also practice navigating around the screen.

Navigation Practice
1. Click on the Ribbon Toolbar menu at the top of the screen, click on all the tabs and observe which commands are located on each tab:

2. When you load Add-Ins you will see an extra **Add-Ins** tab:

3. Right-click on the Ribbon Toolbar and display the Ribbon Toolbar Menu:

4. To allow more buttons to be displayed on the **Quick Access Toolbar**, click on the **Show Quick Access Toolbar Below the Ribbon** to move the **Quick Access Toolbar** below the **Ribbon Toolbar**.
5. Click on the **Customise...** to open the **Ribbon Customisation** form. Explore the tabs on the left-hand side.
6. The Eastwood Harris Asta Powerproject Version 15 Quick Access Toolbar has been created to make using Powerproject simpler. Download this file from www.eh.com.au **Software and Downloads** page, unzip it by double clicking on it and dragging the XML file to your desktop.
7. Then import the toolbar into Asta by right clicking on your Asta Quick Access toolbar to open the **Ribbon Customisation** form and selecting **Customise...**, **Ribbon**, **Import/Export**.
8. Right-click on the Ribbon Toolbar and display the Ribbon Toolbar Menu. Click on **Minimise the Ribbon** to hide the Ribbon Toolbar.
9. Click in a column header to display a double headed arrow and move the column to a different position by dragging.
10. Resize the Date Zone (timescale) by clicking on a tick mark in the **Date Zone** to display a double headed arrow and dragging left and right.
11. Move the Date Zone left and right by left clicking in the timescale and when the Hand icon is displayed drag the timescale left and right.

12. Right Click in the Gantt Chart and select **Properties View** to split the screen:

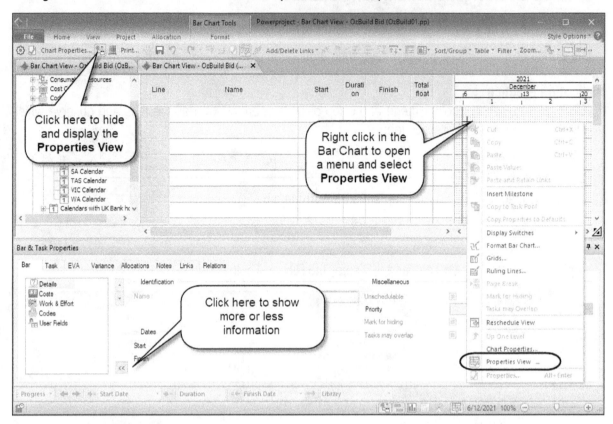

13. Click on the show more and less information button.
14. Close the **Properties View**.
15. Right Click in the Gantt Chart and you will notice the **Properties** button is grey. You will need to add a task before you may open the **Properties** form.
16. Click on the **Projects View** button to hide and display the **Projects View,** this is where you access the calendars, resources and codes etc.

Workshop 3 – Maintaining the Calendars

Background

The normal working week at OzBuild Ltd is Monday to Friday, 8 hours per day excluding Public Holidays. The installation staff work Monday to Saturday, 8 hours per day.

Assignment
The company observes the following holidays:

	2019	2020	2021	2022
New Year's Day	1 January	1 January	1 January	3 January*
Easter	19 – 22 April	10 – 13 April	2 – 5 April	15 – 18 April
Christmas Day	25 December	25 December	27 December*	27 December*
Boxing Day	26December	28 December*	28December*	26December

* These holidays occur on a weekend and the dates in the table above have been moved to the next weekday.

NOTE: Boxing Day, the day after Christmas, is a holiday celebrated in many countries.

Assignment
1. Open the **Library Explorer**.
2. Copy and paste an existing 5-day week, 8 hour per day calendar that does not have holidays into the Calendar root directory. You could use the **5 Day Week No Hols** calendar.
3. Rename to create a calendar titled **OzBuild 5 day/week** which has an 8 hour per day.
4. Open the calendar **Properties** form,
5. Assign the holidays for 2021 and 2022 by Clt clicking on all the holidays in each year,

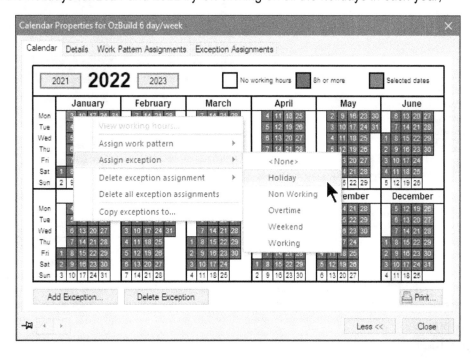

6. Then select **Assign exception**, **Holiday**,
7. Then right click **From work pattern periods** for morning and afternoon and click on **Add**:

8. Delete any holidays not required.
9. Copy and paste the **OzBuild 5 day/week** to create a calendar and name **OzBuild 6 day/week**.
10. Assign the **8hr-day, 6day Week Work Pattern** from the **Calendar Properties**, **Work Pattern Assignments tab.**
11. Add the Easter Saturday Holidays for both 2021 and 2022.
12. Ensure Saturday 25 December 2021 and 1 January 2022 are made into holidays.
13. Close the **Library Explorer**.
14. Make the **OzBuild 5 day/week** calendar the **Task Default** by right clicking on the calendar,
15. Check all the boxes in the **Calendar Settings** form:

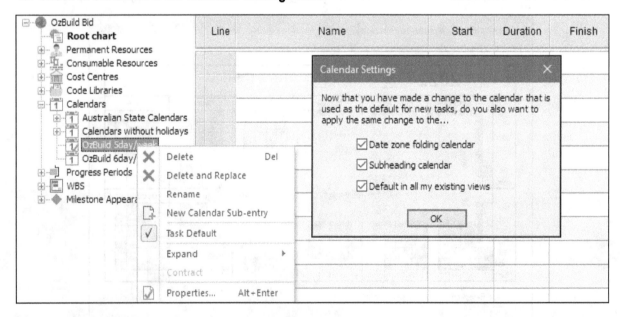

16. Save your project.
17. Check your calendars using the pictures below.

Answers to Workshop 3

OzBuild 5 Day/Week

OzBuild 6 Day/Week

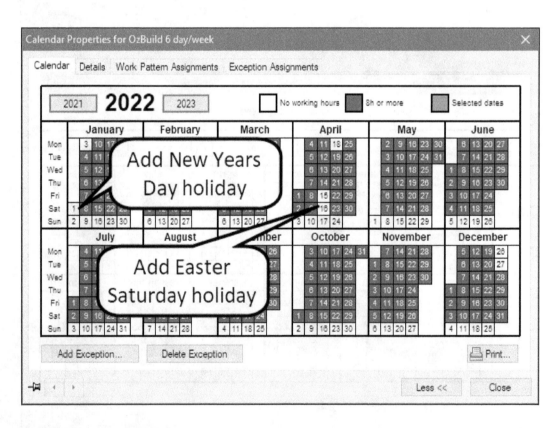

Workshop 4 – Adding Tasks

Background

If you do not use the same template as the one that was used to create the screenshots in this book you may receive a different result.

It is simpler to teach Asta Powerproject by showing how to enter the tasks first and then showing the creation of summary tasks to represent the WBS Nodes or Products or Deliverables second. Once a user understands the process then the tasks and summary tasks may be entered in any order.

Assignment

1. We will assume that the Planning Process is complete and we are to produce a schedule with several tasks for each Product (Deliverable) in the Work Breakdown Structure – WBS.
2. Check the **OzBuild 5 day/week** is set as the **Task Default**:

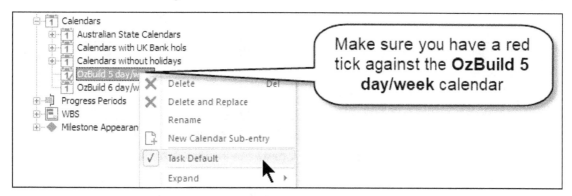

3. If it is not then set it as the **Task Default.**
4. Check all the boxes in the **Calendar Settings** form:

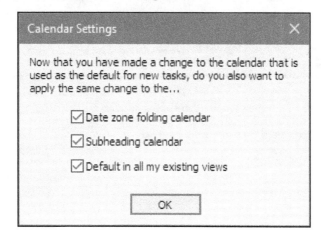

5. Use the columns to enter the Name and Duration of the tasks as below.
6. A task will become a milestone when assigned a zero duration.

ID	Task Name	Duration	Task Calendar
1	Approval to Bid	0 days	
2	Determine Installation Requirements	4 days	
3	Create Technical Specification	5 days	
4	Identify Supplier Components	2 days	
5	Validate Technical Specification	2 days	
6	Document Delivery Methodology	4 days	
7	Obtain Quotes from Suppliers	8 days	
8	Calculate the Bid Estimate	3 days	Assign the 6 Days Working Week calendar
9	Create the Project Schedule	3 days	Assign the 6 Days Working Week calendar
10	Review the Delivery Plan	1 day	
11	Create Draft of Bid Document	6 days	
12	Review Bid Document	4 days	
13	Finalize and Submit Bid Document	2 days	
14	Bid Document Submitted	0 days	Make into a Finish Milestone

7. The estimate and schedule will be completed by site personnel who work a 6-day week.
8. Select the **Calculate the Bid Estimate** and **Create the Project Schedule** task bars or Line Numbers.
9. Assign the OzBuild 6 day/week calendar, drag this calendar onto the selected bars and select the option of **Retain the existing duration and change the dates if necessary**.

10. Do not change the **Folding Calendar**.

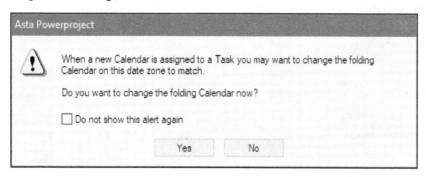

11. Make the Bid Document Submitted into a Finish Milestone by right clicking on the Milestone icon:

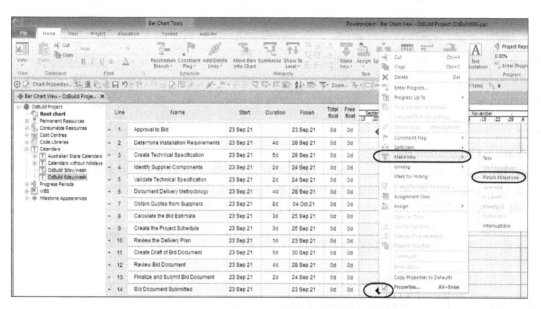

12. Check the calendars in the **Bar and Task Properties** view or form **Task**, **Dates** tab:

13. Press F9 to schedule, if a popup box asks to run a **Reschedule Report** then select **OFF** to cancel it and your schedule should look like this:

Line	Name	Start	Duration	Finish	Total float	Free float
1	Approval to Bid	06 Dec 21		06 Dec 21	8d	8d
2	Determine Installation Requirements	06 Dec 21	4d	09 Dec 21	4d	4d
3	Create Technical Specification	06 Dec 21	5d	10 Dec 21	3d	3d
4	Identify Supplier Components	06 Dec 21	2d	07 Dec 21	6d	6d
5	Validate Technical Specification	06 Dec 21	2d	07 Dec 21	6d	6d
6	Document Delivery Methodology	06 Dec 21	4d	09 Dec 21	4d	4d
7	Obtain Quotes from Suppliers	06 Dec 21	8d	15 Dec 21	0d	0d
8	Calculate the Bid Estimate	06 Dec 21	3d	08 Dec 21	6d	6d
9	Create the Project Schedule	06 Dec 21	3d	08 Dec 21	6d	6d
10	Review the Delivery Plan	06 Dec 21	1d	06 Dec 21	7d	7d
11	Create Draft of Bid Document	06 Dec 21	6d	13 Dec 21	2d	2d
12	Review Bid Document	06 Dec 21	4d	09 Dec 21	4d	4d
13	Finalize and Submit Bid Document	06 Dec 21	2d	07 Dec 21	6d	6d
14	Bid Document Submitted	06 Dec 21		06 Dec 21	8d	8d

14. Save your **OzBuild Bid** project.
15. **Note:** If you are not using the Eastwood Harris template ensure you check you scheduling options are the same as below by selecting **Home**, **Schedule** and from the **Reschedule Branch** drop down list select **Options...**, and ensure that they are as per the picture below:

Workshop 5 - Summary Tasks

Background

The summary tasks may be used to represent a Project, Deliverables/Products, WBS Nodes, Phase, Stages or Work Packages.

We will add summary tasks to represent the Initiation Phase and Deliverables/Products of the Initiation Phase.

Assignment

1. Create a Summary Level 1 for Phase entitled **Bid for Facility Extension** and
2. Create a Summary Level 2 for each of the three Products:
   - **Technical Specification**
   - **Delivery Plan**
   - **Bid Document**
3. Try using the various methods for indenting and outdenting tasks.
4. Your schedule should look like this:

Line	Name	Duration	Start	Finish	Total float	Free float	Calendar
1	⊟ Bid for Facility Extension	8d	06 Dec 21	15 Dec 21	0d	0d	OzBuild 5 day/week
2	⊟ Technical Specification	5d	06 Dec 21	10 Dec 21	3d	3d	OzBuild 5 day/week
3	Approval to Bid		06 Dec 21	06 Dec 21	8d	8d	OzBuild 5 day/week
4	Determine Installation Requirem	4d	06 Dec 21	09 Dec 21	4d	4d	OzBuild 5 day/week
5	Create Technical Specification	5d	06 Dec 21	10 Dec 21	3d	3d	OzBuild 5 day/week
6	Identify Supplier Components	2d	06 Dec 21	07 Dec 21	6d	6d	OzBuild 5 day/week
7	Validate Technical Specification	2d	06 Dec 21	07 Dec 21	6d	6d	OzBuild 5 day/week
8	⊟ Delivery Plan	8d	06 Dec 21	15 Dec 21	0d	0d	OzBuild 5 day/week
9	Document Delivery Methodology	4d	06 Dec 21	09 Dec 21	4d	4d	OzBuild 5 day/week
10	Obtain Quotes from Suppliers	8d	06 Dec 21	15 Dec 21	0d	0d	OzBuild 5 day/week
11	Calculate the Bid Estimate	3d	06 Dec 21	08 Dec 21	6d	6d	OzBuild 6 day/week
12	Create the Project Schedule	3d	06 Dec 21	08 Dec 21	6d	6d	OzBuild 6 day/week
13	Review the Delivery Plan	1d	06 Dec 21	06 Dec 21	7d	7d	OzBuild 5 day/week
14	⊟ Bid Document	6d	06 Dec 21	13 Dec 21	2d	2d	OzBuild 5 day/week
15	Create Draft of Bid Document	6d	06 Dec 21	13 Dec 21	2d	2d	OzBuild 5 day/week
16	Review Bid Document	4d	06 Dec 21	09 Dec 21	4d	4d	OzBuild 5 day/week
17	Finalize and Submit Bid Docume	2d	06 Dec 21	07 Dec 21	6d	6d	OzBuild 5 day/week

5. Use the **Show to** level button to summerise the schedule:

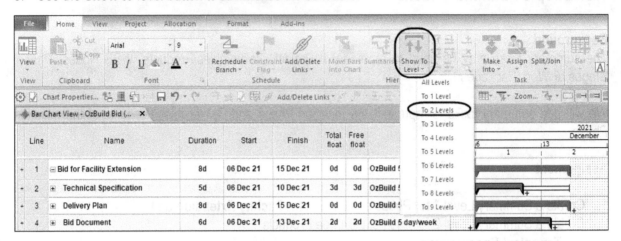

6. Save your **OzBuild Bid** project.
7. **Note:** The Root Chart may be renamed to produce a Level 1 WBS Node.

Workshop 6 - Adding the Links

Background
You have determined the logical sequence of tasks, so you may now enter the links.

Assignment
1. Ensure you have the last workshop file open.
2. Select the **Root Chart** node in the **Project View** so the Line Numbers match the picture below.
3. Input the logic below using several of the methods detailed in this chapter.
4. Use the Zoom Slider at the bottom left hand side of the screen to make the bars larger which in turn makes assigning links graphically easier:

Line	Name	Predecessors	Predecessors
1	⊟ Bid for Facility Extension		
2	⊟ Technical Specification		
3	Approval to Bid		
4	Determine Installation Requirements	3	Approval to Bid
5	Create Technical Specification	4	Determine Installation Requirements
6	Identify Supplier Components	5	Create Technical Specification
7	Validate Technical Specification	6	Identify Supplier Components
8	⊟ Delivery Plan		
9	Document Delivery Methodology	7	Validate Technical Specification
10	Obtain Quotes from Suppliers	6	Identify Supplier Components
11	Calculate the Bid Estimate	9, 10	Document Delivery Methodology, Obtain Quotes from Suppliers
12	Create the Project Schedule	11	Calculate the Bid Estimate
13	Review the Delivery Plan	12	Create the Project Schedule
14	⊟ Bid Document		
15	Create Draft of Bid Document	9	Document Delivery Methodology
16	Review Bid Document	13, 15	Review the Delivery Plan, Create Draft of Bid Document
17	Finalize and Submit Bid Document	16	Review Bid Document
18	Bid Document Submitted	17	Finalize and Submit Bid Document

5. You may wish to apply a **Logic View** to add and review your logic. If you apply **Logic Table** then the date formatting will be reformatted to your system formatting:

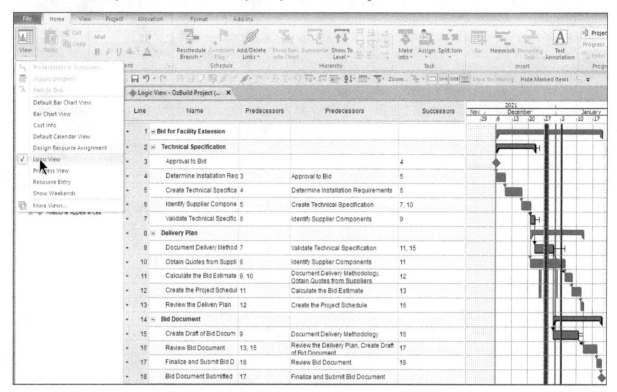

6. Press F9 to calculate the schedule, and accept the defaults:

7. Accept the defaults and click OK.
8. If you receive a schedule report warning, you may wish to click on **Off** so you are not presented with the report in the future.
9. You will end up with multiple tabs open and you may close any you do not need:

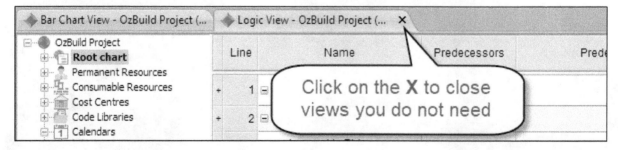

10. You should reapply the Bar Char View and check your dates.

11. If you lose the date formatting this will be because the date formatting is saved with the View and not the Table or you are using a different template. You may reformat the dates by either:

    a. Re applying the **Bar Chart** View, or

    b. Right clicking on the Start and Finish column headers and open the **Format Cells** form:

12. Save your OzBuild Bid project.

Workshop 7 – Constraints

Background

Management has provided further input to your schedule and the client requires the submission on or before the 27 Jan 22.

Assignment

1. Observe the calculated finish and the Critical Path before applying any constraints.

2. Apply a **Finish on or Before** constraint (also known as a **Finish No Later Than** and a **Late Finish** constraint) with a constraint date of 27 Jan 22 to task **Bid Document Submitted** task.

3. If you are presented with an error message, read the message carefully and then set the constraint. Now review float, there should be no change in the Total Float. This demonstrates that a **Finish on or Before** constraint is after the calculated early finish date does not create positive float.

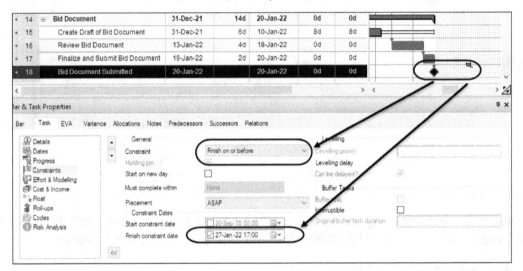

4. Open the **Schedule Options** form and ensure that **Negative float applies to chain** is **NOT** checked:

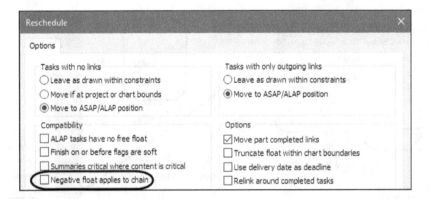

5. Due to proximity to Christmas, management has requested we delay task **Obtain Quotes from Suppliers** until first thing in the New Year, 04 Jan 16. It is hoped that lower prices will be obtained after the Christmas rush.

6. To achieve this, set a **Start on or after** constraint (also known as a **Start No Earlier Than** or **Early Start**) and a constraint date of 04 Jan 22 on task **Obtain Quotes from Suppliers**.

7. You may record this decision in the task notes.

8. Press F9 to reschedule.

9. Should you be presented with an error message,

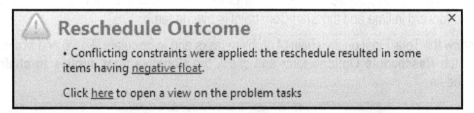

10. Select "**here**" and a new widow will be presented with a new **Reschedule View** one problem activity highlighted:

11. When the **Schedule Options** have **Negative float applies to chain** is **NOT** checked, then the software **DOES NOT** calculate like P6 and Microsoft Project and will only display the first problem task with negative float and a negative float bar.

12. Close the **Reschedule** tab and observe the impact on the Critical Path and end dates.

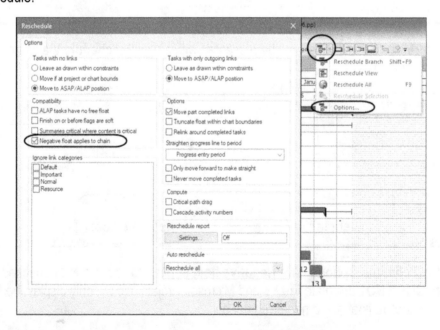

Line	Name	Start	Duration	Finish	Total float	Free float
1	⊟ Bid for Facility Extension	06-Dec-21	36d	27-Jan-22	0d	0d
2	⊟ Technical Specification	06-Dec-21	13d	22-Dec-21	23d	0d
3	Approval to Bid	06-Dec-21		06-Dec-21	5d	0d
4	Determine Installation Requirement	06-Dec-21	4d	09-Dec-21	5d	0d
5	Create Technical Specification	10-Dec-21	5d	16-Dec-21	5d	0d
6	Identify Supplier Components	17-Dec-21	2d	20-Dec-21	5d	0d
7	Validate Technical Specification	21-Dec-21	2d	22-Dec-21	7d	0d
8	⊟ Delivery Plan	23-Dec-21	17d	19-Jan-22	36d	30d
9	Document Delivery Methodology	23-Dec-21	4d	30-Dec-21	7d	0d
10	Obtain Quotes from Suppliers	30-Dec-21	8d	11-Jan-22	-2d	0d
11	Calculate the Bid Estimate	12-Jan-22	3d	14-Jan-22	0d	0d
12	Create the Project Schedule	15-Jan-22	3d	18-Jan-22	0d	0d
13	Review the Delivery Plan	19-Jan-22	1d	19-Jan-22	0d	0d
14	⊟ Bid Document	31-Dec-21	19d	27-Jan-22	36d	36d
15	Create Draft of Bid Document	31-Dec-21	6d	10-Jan-22	7d	7d
16	Review Bid Document	20-Jan-22	4d	25-Jan-22	0d	0d
17	Finalize and Submit Bid Document	26-Jan-22	2d	27-Jan-22	0d	0d
18	Bid Document Submitted	27-Jan-22		27-Jan-22	0d	0d

13. There is 2 days negative float on the **Obtain Quotes from Suppliers** which is scheduled to start on 30 Dec 18 the **Bid Document Submitted** is scheduled on the constraint date and this is not how P6 and Microsoft Project schedules. Finish Constraint acts like a hard constraint and tasks are moved forward in time and the Start Constraint is overridden.

14. To show the Total Float on the chain of problem tasks and to calculate like P6 and Microsoft Project open the **Reschedule Options** form and check the **Negative float applies to chain** and then reschedule.

15. Reschedule.

16. The programme will calculate Total Float and dates like Microsoft Project or P6. The Start Constraint is acknowledged, and the Finish Constraint overridden. There is 2 days negative float on the **Obtain Quotes from Suppliers** which is scheduled to start on 4 Jan 19, the constraint date, and the **Bid Document Submitted** is scheduled on 31 Jan 19. The Reschedule tab shows negative float against the chain of problem tasks in the spreadsheet but the Gantt Chart will **NOT** show a Negative Float bar against any of the tasks:

Line	Name	Start	Duration	Finish	Total float	Free float
1	⊟ Delivery Plan	23-Dec-21	19d	21-Jan-22	-2d	0d
2	Obtain Quotes from Suppli	04-Jan-22	8d	13-Jan-22	-2d	0d
3	Calculate the Bid Estimate	14-Jan-22	3d	17-Jan-22	-2d	0d
4	Create the Project Schedul	18-Jan-22	3d	20-Jan-22	-2d	0d
5	Review the Delivery Plan	21-Jan-22	1d	21-Jan-22	-2d	0d
6	Review Bid Document	24-Jan-22	4d	27-Jan-22	-2d	0d
7	Finalize and Submit Bid Do	28-Jan-22	2d	31-Jan-22	-2d	0d
8	Bid Document Submitted	31-Jan-22		31-Jan-22	-2d	0d

17. **Note:** The author has raised an enhancement request with Asta to display the Negative Float Bar against all tasks with negative float when **Negative float applies to chain** is checked.

18. After review, it is agreed that 2 days can be deducted from task Review Bid Document. Change the duration of this task to 2 days.

19. Reschedule and you will notice that the Total Float of all critical tasks is now zero and the Critical Path runs between the two tasks with constraints.

Line	Name	Start	Duration	Finish	Total float	Free float
1	⊟ Bid for Facility Extension	06-Dec-21	36d	27-Jan-22	0d	0d
2	⊟ Technical Specification	06-Dec-21	13d	22-Dec-21	9d	0d
3	Approval to Bid	06-Dec-21		06-Dec-21	7d	0d
4	Determine Installation	06-Dec-21	4d	09-Dec-21	7d	0d
5	Create Technical Specifi	10-Dec-21	5d	16-Dec-21	7d	0d
6	Identify Supplier Compo	17-Dec-21	2d	20-Dec-21	7d	0d
7	Validate Technical Speci	21-Dec-21	2d	22-Dec-21	9d	0d
8	⊟ Delivery Plan	23-Dec-21	19d	21-Jan-22	0d	0d
9	Document Delivery Meth	23-Dec-21	4d	30-Dec-21	9d	0d
10	Obtain Quotes from Sup	04-Jan-22	8d	13-Jan-22	0d	0d
11	Calculate the Bid Estim	14-Jan-22	3d	17-Jan-22	0d	0d
12	Create the Project Sche	18-Jan-22	3d	20-Jan-22	0d	0d
13	Review the Delivery Pla	21-Jan-22	1d	21-Jan-22	0d	0d
14	⊟ Bid Document	31-Dec-21	19d	27-Jan-22	0d	0d
15	Create Draft of Bid Docu	31-Dec-21	6d	10-Jan-22	13d	13d
16	Review Bid Document	24-Jan-22	2d	25-Jan-22	0d	0d
17	Finalize and Submit Bid	26-Jan-22	2d	27-Jan-22	0d	0d
18	Bid Document Submitte	27-Jan-22		27-Jan-22	0d	0d

20. You may end up with a number of tabs open and it is suggested you close all the ones you do not need.

21. Save your **OzBuild Bid** project.

Workshop 8 - Other task Types

You will go through the process of creating the following in your schedule:

- Task-per-line mode
- Expanded Tasks
- Hammock Tasks
- Task Names as Headers Only

Task-per-line mode

1. Select the second blank line after your last task.
2. Draw 5 tasks on your Gantt chart which have the duration of 5, 2, 1, 7 and 1 day long on one line,
3. Enter a Name of **Concrete Pour**:

4. Click on the + sign to the left of the Line No and type in the new task names:

5. Assign a 7 day per week calendar to the Cure task, accept the default and DO NOT change the Folding Calendar.

6. You will see the schedule shortens and there are no holidays shown for the Cure task because Powerproject displays the Non Work time against each task:

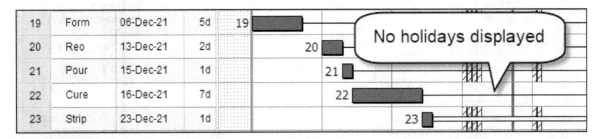

Note: There are no links and they have an inherited Finish to Start link.

Expanded Tasks

1. Add a new task named **Concrete Pour** in the second blank line below your last task with a duration of 5 days,
2. Right click and select **Make Into** and **Expanded** task:

3. Double click on the Expanded task bar to open a new window,
4. Add the same five tasks, link them and assign the 7 day per week to the Cure task, do not change the Folding Calendar.

5. Open the **Project View** and expand the heading **Root Chart**.
6. Click on the all the headings individually from OzBuild to Concrete Pour and you will see how the **Root Chart** works and how **Expanded Task** operate.
7. Select **Root Chart** and **Concrete Pour** in the Project View and see that the Expanded Concrete Pour activities are below the Expanded task.
8. Select **Bid for Facility Extension** and **Concrete Pour** in the Project View and see that the Expanded Concrete Pour activities are at the bottom of the list of tasks:

Hammock Tasks

1. Select the **Root Chart** heading,
2. Add a task in the second blank line below your last task named **Supplier Involvement** and assign a duration of 5d,
3. Right click on the bar and select **Make Into**, **Hammock**:

4. Note the change in shape of the Hammock bar,
5. Select the task bars for Identify Supplier Components, Obtain Quotes from Suppliers and Create the Project Schedule.
6. Right click and select **Add to Hammock**, select the **Supplier Involvement** task and select OK:

7. Your schedule should look like this:

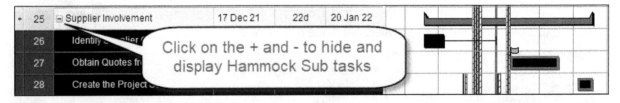

Click on the + and - to hide and display Hammock Sub tasks

8. The tasks that are part of the Hammock may be seen twice, once in the schedule and once under the Hammock.

---

9. Click on the sign to the left of the Hammock name to hide or display the Hammock sub tasks:

Task Names as Headers Only

10. When a blank line is created and only a Name is entered and no duration then this becomes a heading only.

11. The picture below shows two headings titled Concrete Pour 1 and Concrete Pour 2, and they have no bar in the Gantt chart:

12. Now delete all the tasks you have created in this workshop:

- Task-per-line mode,

- Expanded Tasks,

- Hammock Tasks, ensure you do not select the Hammock sub tasks.

Workshop 9 - Formatting the Bar Chart

Background

Management has received your draft report and requests some changes to the presentation.

Assignment

Format your schedule as follows:

1. Add a date line **Date (1-31)** to the **Date Zone** by Right Clicking in the **Date Zone** and selecting **Properties**:

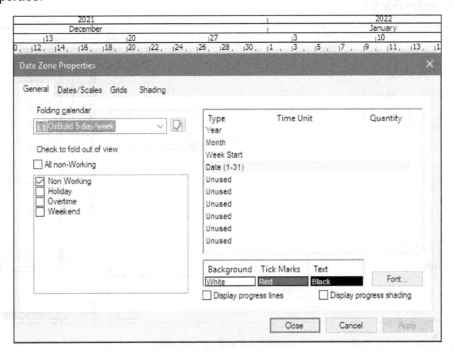

2. Display the **Elapsed Day** Gridline against all Date Zones:

3. Slice the **Date Zone** twice by Right Clicking in the Timescale and selecting **Start New Scale Zone**:

4. Then adjust each zone to a different scale.

5. Remove the Time Zones by Right Clicking in the Timescale on the new Time Zones and selecting **Remove This Scale Zone**:

6. Select the **General** tab, ensure the **Folding calendar** is the **OzBuild 5 day/week** and hide **All non-Working** time, you will see the Non-Work days are hidden:

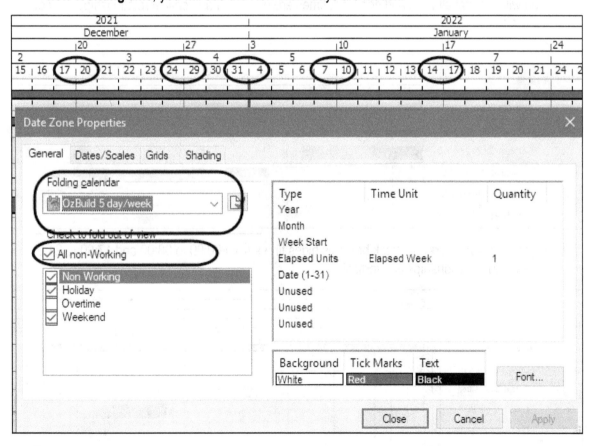

7.   Now unclick all **Check fold out of view** options:

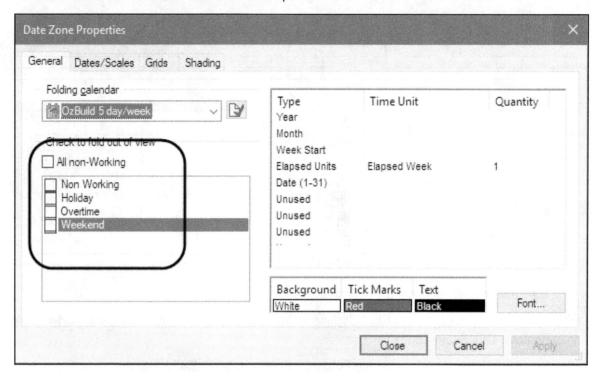

8.   You will see that all work and non work times are dispalyed and critical relationships are not vertical:

9.   Check the **Non Working** check box, this hides times from 00:00 to 08:00 and 17:00 to 24:00.
10. Now driving relationships are vertical:

11. Check the **Holiday**, this will hide Holidays:

12. Uncheck **Holiday** and check **Weekend** to hide the weekends:

13. Use the Critical, Free Float and Total Float buttons to hde and display these bars:

14. Add the **Calendar** column and some other coumns such as Predecessors by right clicking on a heading and selecting **Add Column**, **Date**, **Calendar**:

15. Remove the Columns.

16. Save your project.

Workshop 10 - Code Libraries

Background
We want to issue reports for comment by management by assigning responsibility to the activities and producing reports for each person.

Assignment
1. Creating a Responsibility Code,
    - Click on the **Open the Library Explorer** button to open the **Library Explorer**,
    - Add a **Responsibility** Code Library, and
    - Add three Codes with different display formatting for each code:
        - Angela Lowe - Purchasing
        - Carol Peterson - Bid Manager
        - Scott Morrison - Engineering

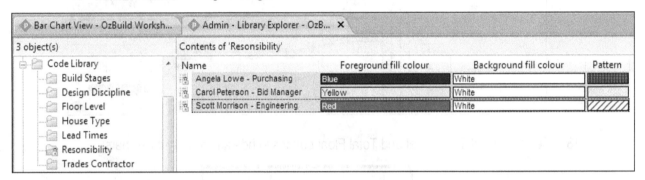

2. Assign the Responsibilities in the table below by clicking on the bars and dragging from the **Project View** or adding the **Task Responsibility** column:

ID	Task Name	Responsibility
1	**Bid for Facility Extension**	
2	**Technical Specification**	
3	Approval to Bid	
4	Determine Installation Requirements	Scott Morrison - Engineering
5	Create Technical Specification	Scott Morrison - Engineering
6	Identify Supplier Components	Angela Lowe - Purchasing
7	Validate Technical Specification	Scott Morrison - Engineering
8	**Delivery Plan**	
9	Document Delivery Methodology	Scott Morrison - Engineering
10	Obtain Quotes from Suppliers	Angela Lowe - Purchasing
11	Calculate the Bid Estimate	Scott Morrison - Engineering
12	Create the Project Schedule	Carol Peterson - Bid Manager
13	Review the Delivery Plan	Carol Peterson - Bid Manager
14	**Bid Document**	
15	Create Draft of Bid Document	Carol Peterson - Bid Manager
16	Review Bid Document	Carol Peterson - Bid Manager
17	Finalize and Submit Bid Document	Carol Peterson - Bid Manager
18	Bid Document Submitted	

3. Click **Yes** when you receive the message below:

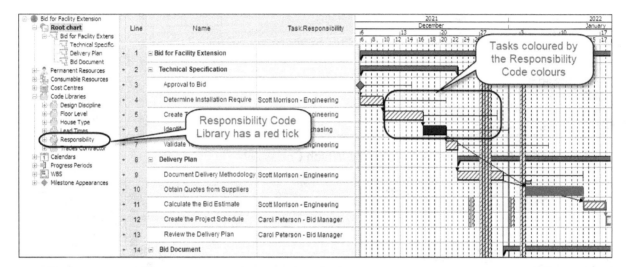

4. Now select **View**, **View Data** group, **Filter**, select **Which Code?** and produce a report for each responsible person:

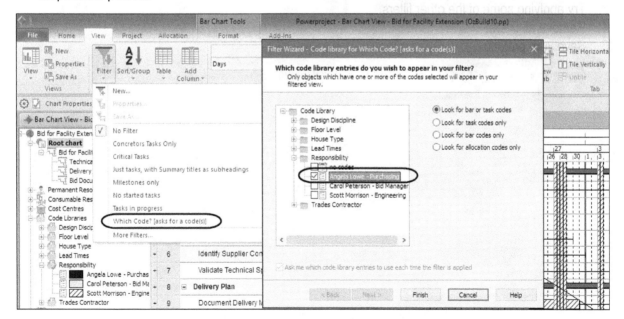

5. Remove all filters and any additional columns you have added, such as Responsibility and Calendar.
6. Save your **OzBuild Bid** project.

Workshop 11 – Filters

Background
Management has asked for some reports to suit their unique requirements.

Assignment
1. They would like to see all the critical tasks so apply the Critical Filter:

2. Now filter on Angela Lowes tasks using the **Which Code** filter.

3. Try applying some of the other filters,
4. Remove all filters,
5. Save your project.

Workshop 12 - Organizing Tasks Using Group and Sort

Background
Having completed the schedule, you want to report the project schedule with different views.

Assignment
Create a Sort/Group to group the tasks by Responsibility:
1. From the **View** tab, select **Sort/Group**,
2. Click on **New**,
3. Enter a name for this sort, e.g. **Responsibility**,
4. Do not select a category for this sort,
5. In the Type column, select **Task**,
6. In the Attribute column select **Responsibility**,

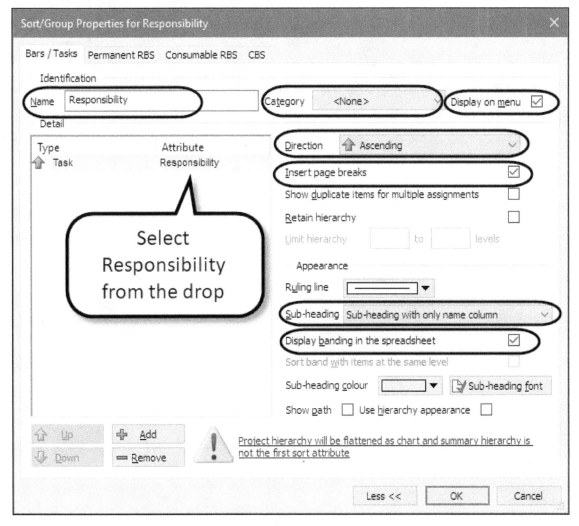

7. Tick Insert page break to have a page break at the bottom of each set of data. This will allow you to print each set of data on a separate page,
8. The Sub-heading drop down allows you to choose how you want the summary heading to be displayed, select **Subheading with only name column**,
9. Change the **Sub-heading font** to Ariel Bold 10.

---

10. Click OK to apply the sort,
11. Apply the **Task Only** filter to remove the summary tasks:

Line	Name	Task Responsibility	Start	Duration	Finish
	⊟ **Angela Lowe - Purchasing**				
1	Identify Supplier Components	Angela Lowe - Purchasing	17 Dec 21	2d	20 Dec 21
2	Obtain Quotes from Suppliers	Angela Lowe - Purchasing	04 Jan 22	8d	13 Jan 22
	⊟ **Carol Peterson - Bid Manager**				
3	Create the Project Schedule	Carol Peterson - Bid Manager	18 Jan 22	3d	20 Jan 22
4	Review the Delivery Plan	Carol Peterson - Bid Manager	21 Jan 22	1d	21 Jan 22
5	Create Draft of Bid Document	Carol Peterson - Bid Manager	31 Dec 21	6d	10 Jan 22
6	Review Bid Document	Carol Peterson - Bid Manager	24 Jan 22	2d	25 Jan 22
7	Finalize and Submit Bid Document	Carol Peterson - Bid Manager	26 Jan 22	2d	27 Jan 22
	⊟ **Scott Morrison - Engineering**				
8	Determine Installation Requirement	Scott Morrison - Engineering	06 Dec 21	4d	09 Dec 21
9	Create Technical Specification	Scott Morrison - Engineering	10 Dec 21	5d	16 Dec 21
10	Validate Technical Specification	Scott Morrison - Engineering	21 Dec 21	2d	22 Dec 21
11	Document Delivery Methodology	Scott Morrison - Engineering	23 Dec 21	4d	30 Dec 21
12	Calculate the Bid Estimate	Scott Morrison - Engineering	14 Jan 22	3d	17 Jan 22

12. Remove the Group and by selecting **Natural Order**
13. Remover the Filter,
14. Save your file.

Workshop 13 – Printing

Background
We want to issue a report for comment by management.

Assignment
1. Apply the **Bar Chart View**, and remove any additional columns you have added so there are only the Line, Name, Start, Duration, Finish Total Float and Free Float columns displayed.
2. Select **File**, **Print**, **Options**.
3. Select A3 Landscape, or paper size that your country usually uses,
4. Select the Boarder file **CHT-A3L.B: A3 Landscape PowerDraw Generated** if available, or a boarder to suit your selected paper size:

5. View the result:

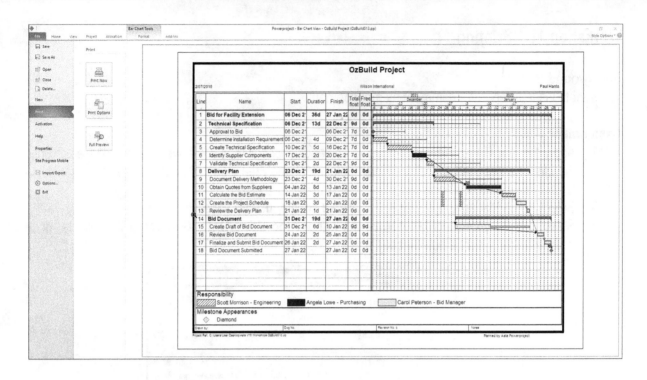

Workshop 14 - Setting a Baseline

Background
It is at the end of the first week you have to update the schedule to report progress and slippage.

Assignment
Open your **OzBuild Bid** project file and complete the following steps:

1. Set the Baseline for all the tasks on your project using the **Project, Properties** group, **Baseline Manager, New...** command and give the Baseline a name of **Contract Baseline**.
2. Apply the **Progress View** by selecting **View, Views** group, View and select **Progress View** from the drop-down list.
3. You will now have two views open and two tabs at the top of the Gannt Chart.
4. Select **Format, Format** group, **Format Bar Chart**, select the **Baselines** tab and check the box **Check to show for...** to display the baseline bars. At this point in time both the Contract and Current Baseline will be the same:

5. You should see the Baseline Bars below the current schedule, but your column formats may be different, but may be reformatted using the **Format Cells** command:

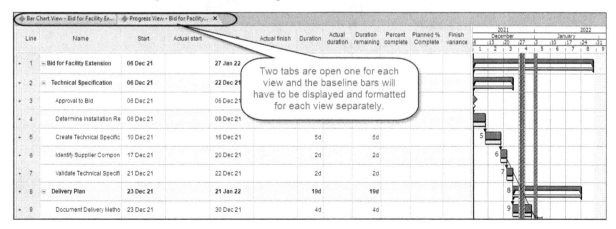

Workshop 15 - Updating an Unsourced Project

1. In this workshop we will only use one Report Date and use the Progress View.
2. Open the **Project View** by clicking on the **Project View** button on the Quick Access Toolbar,
3. Open the **Progress Period Propperties for Project Report Date** form and change the **Project Report Dates to** 13 December 2021:

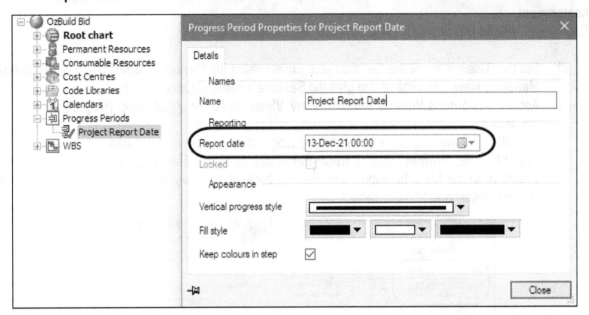

4. Open the **Format Bar Chart** form, select the **Progress** tab and ensure the boxes as per below are checked:

5. Select the **Baseline** tab and ensure the **Current Baseline** is displayed, this will be the same as the Contract Baseline at this point in time:

6. You should now see a Jagged Report Line and the Planned % Complete has been calculated:

7. Expand the time scale as required to see the detail.
8. Ensure your columns are as per below.

Line	Name	Start	Actual start	Finish	Actual finish	Duration	Actual duration	Duration remaining	Percent complete	Planned % Complete	Finish variance

9. For clarity add the Grids for Elapsed Days and Date Zone time units of Day (1-31).
10. Select the **Root chart** and update the following tasks using the table below. Enter the data in the exact order below against the detail tasks only:
   - Task 3 - Actual Start of 07-Dec-21, it should also show 100 % against the Milestones,
   - Task 4 - Actual Start of 07-Dec-21and Actual Finish of 9-Dec-21, it should now show 100%,
   - Task 5 - Actual Start of 09-Dec-21 and enter a % Complete of 20%. You will see the Actual Duration is calculated for you and there is a Jagged Progress Line:

11. You will notice there is a Jagged Progress Line with incomplete progress in the past,
12. Press F9 to schedule,
13. Task 5 has now been split.

Line	Name	Start	Actual start	Finish	Actual finish	Duration	Actual duration	Duration remaining	Percent complete	Planned % Complete	Finish variance	
1	⊟ Bid for Facilit	07-Dec-21	07-Dec-21	27-Jan-22		35d	4d	31d	9.76	11.90		
2	⊟ Technical S	07-Dec-21	07-Dec-21	22-Dec-21		12d	4d	8d	33.33	38.46		
3	Approval t	07-Dec-21	07-Dec-21	07-Dec-21	07-Dec-21				100.00	100.00	-1d	
4	Determin	07-Dec-21	07-Dec-21	09-Dec-21	09-Dec-21	3d	3d		100.00	100.00		
5	Create Te	09-Dec-21	09-Dec-21	16-Dec-21		5d	1d	4d	20.00	20.00		
6	Identify Su	17-Dec-21		20-Dec-21		2d		2d				

14. At this point in time the **Remaining Duration** is calculated from the **Progress Date**.
15. Task 5 - change the Remaining Duration to 6 days and reschedule.

Line	Name	Start	Actual start	Finish	Actual finish	Duration	Actual duration	Duration remaining	Percent complete	Planned % Complete	Finish variance	
1	⊟ Bid for Facilit	07-Dec-21	07-Dec-21	27-Jan-22		35d	4d	31d	9.30	11.90		
2	⊟ Technical S	07-Dec-21	07-Dec-21	24-Dec-21		14d	4d	10d	28.57	38.46	-2d	
3	Approval t	07-Dec-21	07-Dec-21	07-Dec-21	07-Dec-21				100.00	100.00	-1d	
4	Determin	07-Dec-21	07-Dec-21	09-Dec-21	09-Dec-21	3d	3d		100.00	100.00		
5	Create Te	09-Dec-21	09-Dec-21	20-Dec-21		7d	1d	6d	14.29	20.00	-2d	
6	Identify Su	21-Dec-21		22-Dec-21		2d		2d			-2d	

16. NOTE: there is no change in the end date of the project as there is enough Float to absorb the delay.
17. Save your OzBuild Bid project.

Workshop 16 - Library Explorer

1. Display the **Library Explorer** and open the **Show Libraries** form.

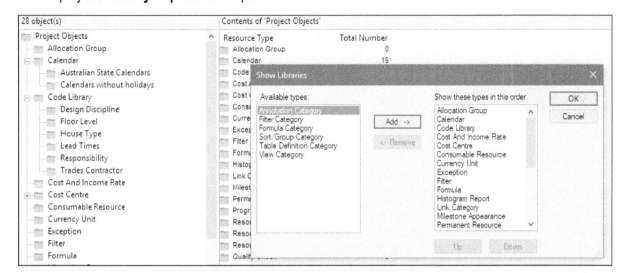

2. Ensure only Category fields are NOT displayed and they are therefore listed under **Available Types**,
3. Reorder the displayed heading alphabetically,
4. Close the **Show Libraries** form,
5. Check your results and then close the Library Explorer.

Course Agenda and PowerPoint Slides

Day 1 - Create an Unresourced Project

1. Introduction to Asta Powerproject and Creating a project

2. Navigation and Setting Options

3. Calendars

4. Tasks and Milestones

5. Summary Tasks

6. Linking Tasks to create a Critical Path Schedule and Reschedule

7. Constraints

8. Other Task Types

Day 2 – Formatting, Reports and Updating an Unresourced Project

9. Formatting the Display

10. Code Libraries

11. Filters

12. Organising Tasks using Group and Sorts

13. Printing and Reports

14. Baselines

15. Updating an Unresourced Project

16. Library Explorer

17. User Definable Fields and WBS.

EASTWOODHARRIS

CREATE AND UPDATE AN UNRESOURCED PROJECT USING ASTA POWERPROJECT

VERSION 15

1

EASTWOOD HARRIS PTY LTD.

Welcome to the
**Create and Update an
Unresourced Project
using
Elecosoft (Asta) Powerproject
Version 15**
training course

Page 2

2

EASTWOOD HARRIS PTY LTD.

Administration

- Evacuation and First Aid,
- Facilities, timings and meals,
- Mobile phones & emails,
- Introductions:
  - Your name,
  - The types of projects you are involved in,
  - Your experience in scheduling software, and
  - What you intend to do with the software after the course,
- Course attendance sheet.

Page 3   3

Copyright Eastwood Harris Pty Ltd 2020

3

EASTWOOD HARRIS PTY LTD.

Required background to attend this course

To attend this course you are expected to:

- Understand how projects are managed and the project management process required to run projects,
- Understand how to use PCs and the operating system,
- A basic understanding of Critical Path concepts, including how the forward and backward pass calculate Early Dates, Late Dates, the Critical Path and Float,
- Experience in using project planning and scheduling software such as Microsoft Project or Primavera P6, etc. would be beneficial but not essential.

Page 4   4

Copyright Eastwood Harris Pty Ltd 2020

4

EASTWOOD HARRIS PTY LTD.

Course Objectives

This objectives of this course are to teach participants:

- The user interface,
- How to create a project,
- Scheduling projects without resources,
- Filters, Views, Sorts and Printing,
- Creating and assigning a baseline and
- Updating an un-resourced project,

Successful completion of all the course workshops will confirm that the objectives have been met,

Note: Powerproject has a large amount of functionality and this course does not cover all aspects of the software. Please refer to the help files for a more detailed understanding of the functions not covered.

5

EASTWOOD HARRIS PTY LTD.

Course Conduct

- This course is instructor lead,
- The instructor will demonstrate the software with a combination of PowerPoint presentations and live software demonstrations,
- Most topics are reinforced by workshops,
- The manual is yours to take away,
- Take any notes,
- Ask any questions.

6

EASTWOOD HARRIS PTY LTD.

Course Agenda

Day 1 - Create an Unresourced Project

1. Introduction to Powerproject and Creating a project
2. Navigation and Setting Options
3. Calendars
4. Tasks and Milestones
5. Summary Tasks
6. Linking Tasks to create a Critical Path Schedule
7. Constraints.

Page 7   7   Copyright Eastwood Harris Pty Ltd 2020

7

EASTWOOD HARRIS PTY LTD.

Course Agenda

Day 2 – Formatting, Reports and Updating an Unresourced Project

8. Other Task Types
9. Formatting the Display
10. Code Libraries
11. Filters
12. Organising Tasks using Sort and Groups
13. Printing and Reports
14. Baselines
15. Updating an Unresourced Project
16. User Definable Fields and WBS.

Page 8   8   Copyright Eastwood Harris Pty Ltd 2020

8

EASTWOOD HARRIS PTY LTD.

1 - INTRODUCTION TO POWERPROJECT

- Asta Powerproject was developed in the UK and is one of the oldest PC project scheduling software packages,
- Asta plc was purchase by Elecosoft plc and the term Asta is no longer used by Elecosoft,
- It is very similar in structure to Microsoft Project and Tables, Views, Grouping and Filters have similar functions,
- It has greater functionality than P6 or Microsoft Project which makes the learning curve longer than for other products,
- P6 and Microsoft Project were developed for IT and Business projects and are missing functions desirable on construction projects that are available with Powerproject,
- Powerproject was developed for the construction industry and is more suitable for building and construction projects,
- It uses some different terminology to US products.

Page 13   13   Copyright Eastwood Harris Pty Ltd 2020

13

EASTWOOD HARRIS PTY LTD.

Powerproject Products

Elecosoft has the following main products and many add on software packages:

- **Powerproject**, the main scheduling engine,
- **Easyplan**, a simplified version of Powerproject limited to 250 activities,
- **Project Viewer**, a free viewer where a schedule may be opened and viewed but not modified,
- **4D Planning** by importing your 3D CAD model,
- **Site Progress Mobile**, an app allowing users to record the progress of their project on their mobile phone,
- **Powerproject Vision** a hosted service that allows all users to create a new project from templates and access the latest version of the project program from any location.

14   Copyright Eastwood Harris Pty Ltd 2020

14

EASTWOOD HARRIS PTY LTD.

Powerproject Modes

Powerproject may be run in several modes:

- Single user opening one Powerproject file,
- Multi users opening one Powerproject file,
- Multiple projects and multiple users accessing one database,
- When multiple users are opening a project then security is set at user and task level with real time updates for other users.

15

Copyright Eastwood Harris Pty Ltd 2020

15

EASTWOOD HARRIS PTY LTD.

Powerproject Addon Software

Powerproject has a number of addons that users may download from the Powerproject support website:

- **Addon to move code library items into different libraries** which solves the issue multiple Code assignment to one task which may not be exported to P6,
- **XER Update addon for Primavera P6 baseline imports** to enable Powerproject to import a XER P6 Baseline,
- **Project Comparison** for comparing two projects for changes and forensic analysis,
- **Progress Tools** a collection of tools for examining, transferring or modifying progress,
- **Standard Data Exchange Format (SDEF) Exporter** for the US Military,
- **Predecessor / successor report addon**
- **Lean Construction Suite**
- **BidCon importer for Powerproject**

Copyright Eastwood Harris Pty Ltd 2020

16

EASTWOOD HARRIS PTY LTD.

What is new in Powerproject Version 15 – 1/3

- Interface Refresh with a change in the look of toolbar icons,

- Schedule Quality Check (SQC) allows the schedule checking to ensure it complies with industry or corporate standards,

- Milestone shape library allowing different milestone shapes,

- BIM – Build Direction enhancement allowing showing of progress of work,

- Baselines are now saved as part of a project and not a separate file,

- Progress Appearance has more formatting options,

- Print the Code Library Legend may now be printed on every page,

- Improvements to booking data in and out, a new process for booking data in and out of projects when editing remotely.

17

EASTWOOD HARRIS PTY LTD.

What is new in Powerproject Version 15 – 2/3

- Link Chasing allowing double clicking on a link to chase the path of predecessors and successors,

- Calendar View, a new view similar to the Microsoft Project Calendar view,

- Display Codes from multiple libraries on activities, earlier versions only allowed one Code Library to be displayed,

- Select multiple objects in the Bar Chart using an Area Select Tool,

- Duplicate the links from outside a group of tasks on Copy/Paste allowing the duplication of "External" Links if they are required,

- Display an indicator in the spreadsheet to identify the status of tasks, similar to P6 with an icon showing if an activity is critical or not critical, not started, in progress or complete.

18

EASTWOOD HARRIS PTY LTD.

What is new in Powerproject Version 15 – 3/3

- Task-Work can now be graphed in a similar way to resources,

- Link From/To dialog enhancement that may be used to link multiple tasks at once,

- Group tasks or allocations in sorted/grouped views by day, week, month, quarter or year in the same way as Microsoft Project or P6,

- Enter dated notes against tasks and link documents or webpages to tasks,

- Import from and export to Primavera P6 in XML (as well as XER) format,

- The Version 15 Ribbon Toolbar has some new functions and importing a Version 14 toolbar will remove the new functions from the Ribbon toolbar. It is recommended that a new toolbar is developed from a Version 15 toolbar and exported for others to use.

19

EASTWOOD HARRIS PTY LTD.

What to do when upgrading to Powerproject Version 15 - 1/2

If you are updating a Version 14 template to Version 15 then there are some library items you that need to copy from an existing Powerproject Version 15 template, such as the Powerproject Construction Template, to enable some new functions to operate, including:

- The **Histogram Report**, **Total Task Work**, and

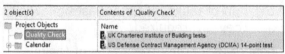

- The two **Quality Check** items,

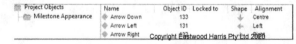

- You should also check that the 30 or so **Milestone Appearance** entries are all present:

Project Objects	Name	Object ID	Locked to	Shape	Alignment
Milestone Appearance	Arrow Down	133			Centre
	Arrow Left	131			Left
	Arrow Right	132			

20

EASTWOOD HARRIS PTY LTD.

What to do when upgrading to Powerproject Version 15 – 2/2

- If you are have a Powerproject Version 14 toolbar that you users import after loading or updating Powerproject then it is better to take and existing Version 15 toolbar and edit it and not import your old Version 14 toolbar into Version 15,

- This is because the Version 14 toolbar has Ribbon commands for new features that are not on old toolbars and importing an older version toolbar will overwrite the existing Version 15 Ribbon toolbar and delete the new functions.

21

EASTWOOD HARRIS PTY LTD.

Powerproject Terminology

Powerproject has some different terminology to US software:

Powerproject	P6 and Microsoft Project
Live project	Current project
Links	Relationships
Relationship, this is the relationship of detailed tasks to a summary task.	This is equivalent to P6 WBS levels and MPS Outline levels.
Block Linking	Chain Linking
Allocate Resource	Assign Resource
Allocation	Assignment
Date Zone	Timescale
Rulers	Gridlines
Report Date	Data Date – P6 Status Date – Microsoft Project
Imposed start	Project Start Date
Subheading - a description without a Gantt chart bar.	No equivalent.
Annotation	A graphic item added to the Gantt Chart.

22

EASTWOOD HARRIS PTY LTD.

Mouse Clicking and Copy and Paste

1. Powerproject follows many Microsoft Windows conventions:

2. Left click will select an item,

3. Double click will activate it,

4. Right click opens a menu,

5. Click and drag moves a cell or selects multiple items,

6. Shift button allows selection of adjacent items,

7. Control button allows selection of non-adjacent items,

8. Copy and Paste. When copying from a spreadsheet you must select more than one cell in Powerproject before pasting. For example, if you select and copy 6 cells in a spreadsheet then if you select one cell in Powerproject all the data will be pasted into the one Powerproject cell. To paste into 6 cells you must select 2 or more cells in Powerproject before pasting. If you select 12 cells in Powerproject the data will be pasted twice.

23

EASTWOOD HARRIS PTY LTD.

Undo and Redo

- The Powerproject Undo and Redo function does not operate on formatting functions, it only works on edits that affect the schedule calculations and schedule data,

- An Undo is not lost when a project is saved,

- All Undos are lost when a project is closed,

- A list of Undos is available from the dropdown list by the Undo icon:

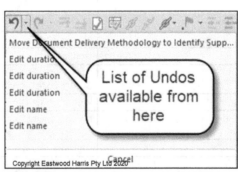

24

EASTWOOD HARRIS PTY LTD.

File Locations

- After opening Powerproject for the first time you will need to set the file locations to suit your requirements,

- To set the Powerproject directories select File, Options, File Locations:

- You will need to save your templates into the Template folder,

- Set your Live and Baseline file directory, these are best set as the same directory, so you do not loose your Baseline files.

- **Note:** The Baseline directory was initially not used in Version 15 and then reinstated.

25

EASTWOOD HARRIS PTY LTD.

File Extensions

Powerproject projects have the following files extensions:

- Live projects (Current project) - *.pp

- Templates - *.pp

- Backup projects - *.bak

- Boarder files used when printing*.b

- Baselines - *.ppb

- **Note:** Version 15 initially would only save the baseline as part of the current project and when earlier versions of a project are opened then the earlier baseline in a *.ppb format will be read. Later versions of Version 15 gave users the option of saving a baseline as a separate file like earlier versions. Baseline files are smaller than a Live project files because they only hold data and no formatting.

26

EASTWOOD HARRIS PTY LTD.

Creating Templates

- Corporate templates are essential when using Powerproject and should include items such as Codes, Calendars, Views, Filters, Border files, Reports and sample task sets,

- To create a Template just save a file in the Template directory that has been selected in File, Options, File Locations, Template project path,

- If you have been upgrading from earlier versions of Powerproject you may find templates in several locations which are all read by Powerproject:

  - c:\program files\

  - c:\program files (x86)\ on 64-bit machines

  - c:\programdata\

  - the users My Documents folder,

- It is recommended that you clean up your templates so they only reside in one directory:

Copyright Eastwood Harris Pty Ltd 2020

27

EASTWOOD HARRIS PTY LTD.

Template Location History

- Powerproject templates are saved in different locations for compatibility reasons:

- Windows XP which does not have newer security restrictions are in the c:\program files\ since it is accessible by all users on the machine,

- With Windows Vista, Microsoft introduced the new security rules preventing user access to c:\program files\ and then Template were set to:

  - Saved in c:\programdata\ if required by all users, or

  - Save in the users My Documents folder if only required by the individual user,

- You may end up with templates in several locations and they are all read by Powerproject irrespective of your File, Locations setting,

- If you wish to delete all Powerproject templates you may need to look in all these locations.

Copyright Eastwood Harris Pty Ltd 2020

28

EASTWOOD HARRIS PTY LTD.

Powerproject Properties Forms

- Powerproject has a number of Properties forms and therefore when you open a Properties form you need to be aware of what Properties form you are opening,

- For example there are:

  - Date Zone Properties

  - Chart Properties

  - Calendar Properties

  - Filter Properties

  - Sort and Group Properties

- Therefore when you are in the Date Zone and right click and select Properties you will open the Date Zone Properties form.

Copyright Eastwood Harris Pty Ltd 2020

29

EASTWOOD HARRIS PTY LTD.

System Date Format

- The date format displayed in Powerproject dialogue boxes, such as the Start Date in the Chart Properties form, is adopted from your System Short Date format,

- You may change your System Short Date from Start, Settings, Time and Language and this will affect dates in many apps such as File Explorer etc.,

- The workshops display the format of dd-MMM-yy and display dates in this format: 31-Dec-21,

- Thus people in the US (that use the format mm-dd-yy, 12-31-21) and most Western countries (that use the format of dd-mm-yy, 31-12-21) will all understand the date formats used in the workshops,

- The formatting of dates of columns is covered in the Formatting section of this course.

Copyright Eastwood Harris Pty Ltd 2020

30

13

Creating a Project

- Templates are used to make creating a new project as simple as possible. Template should contain information that you may wish to use regularly such as tables, code libraries, filters and many more items,

- Select File, New,

- Select a template on which to base your project e.g. Construction Template,

- Enter the project details,

- NOTE: It is very important to create your own organisations templates to save your schedulers from creating the same Filters, Calendars, Currencies and Views over and over again.

Page 31   31

Copyright Eastwood Harris Pty Ltd 2020

31

Opening an existing project

- To open a protect:

- Select File, Open,

- Use the applicable option from this form,

- There is a new option to use Powerproject Vision.

Page 32   32

Copyright Eastwood Harris Pty Ltd 2020

32

EASTWOOD HARRIS PTY LTD.

Importing a Microsoft Project, SureTrak or Primavera P6 Project

- Powerproject will import all of these project file types from the File, Import command:

- MSP files must be saved in XML format unless you have Microsoft Project loaded and then files in MPP format may be imported,

- SureTrak in STX format,

- P6 in XER or XML format,

- NOTE: The projects created by different software will often calculate differently and will often display different dates, costs or units.

Copyright Eastwood Harris Pty Ltd 2020

EASTWOOD HARRIS PTY LTD.

Changing the Project Start Date

- The start date of a selected project may be changed by:

    - Selecting File, Properties, Advanced Properties,

    - Change the Imposed start to the new project start date and click Close:

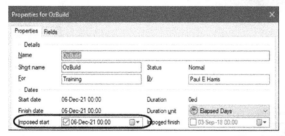

- The date format displayed in Powerproject dialogue boxes, such as the Start Date in the File, New form, is adopted from your System Short Date format,

    - Note: If your project does not move when you have changed your Imposed Start then check your Report Date.

Copyright Eastwood Harris Pty Ltd 2020

EASTWOOD HARRIS PTY LTD.

Selecting the currency

5

- Powerproject templates loaded with the software are often configured with UK Pounds as the currency,
- To change the currency to a different currency:
    - Open the project that you will be working with,
    - Display the Currencies in the Library Explorer,
    - If the currency you require does not exist then add the currency you require or rename an existing currency,
    - Assign your Currency to your project, and
    - Save your new project as a template, so when you create a new project it will have the correct Currency,
- NOTE: One currency is the Base currency and may not be deleted. It has a 5 icon and is used to calculate the rates of all other currencies. This and one other system currency may not be deleted, but they may be renamed.

Page 35 35   Copyright Eastwood Harris Pty Ltd 2020

35

EASTWOOD HARRIS PTY LTD.

Showing the currency in the Library Explorer

- Select **View**, **Library Explorer**, to open the **Library Explorer** in a new window,
- Right click in the bottom left hand window and select Show Libraries...,

- Add the Currency Unit,
- The Library Explorer is covered in more detail later.

Page 36 36   Copyright Eastwood Harris Pty Ltd 2020

36

EASTWOOD HARRIS PTY LTD.

Creating a new currency

- Click on the Currency Unit in the Library Explorer,

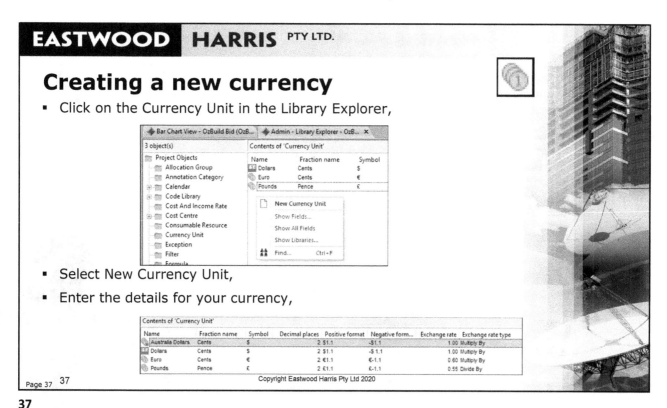

- Select New Currency Unit,
- Enter the details for your currency,

EASTWOOD HARRIS PTY LTD.

Setting the default currency

- Select **File**, **Options**, **View** tab,
- Select your currency under **Default currency**,
- A template should be created with the **default currency** set,
- An Australian and US dollar construction template is available at www.eh.com.au and select Software and Downloads.

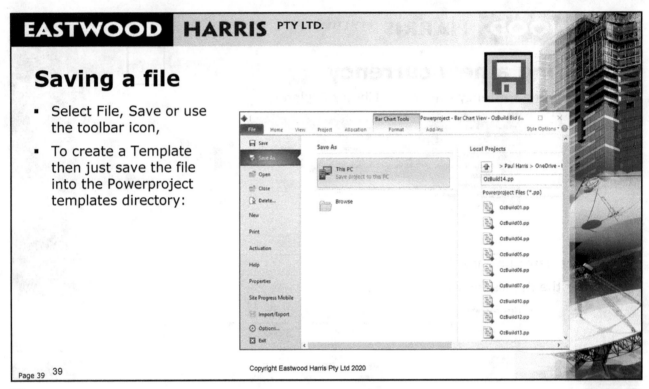

Saving a file

- Select File, Save or use the toolbar icon,

- To create a Template then just save the file into the Powerproject templates directory:

Page 39   39

Copyright Eastwood Harris Pty Ltd 2020

39

Powerproject File Versions

- Powerproject introduces new file formats at times,

- Older versions are automatically converted on opening,

- If you wish to share a project with a user with an earlier version of Powerproject then you will need to use the File, Save As option and select an earlier version:

Page 40   40

Copyright Eastwood Harris Pty Ltd 2020

40

18

EASTWOOD HARRIS PTY LTD.

Saving a file with a new name

- When a file is saved with a new name, the existing version is kept as last saved, and a new version is saved under the new name,

- Select File, Save As, or click on the Save As icon,

- Select the location and name for your file and press Save:

Copyright Eastwood Harris Pty Ltd 2020

41

EASTWOOD HARRIS PTY LTD.

Closing a project

- Select **File**, **Close**,

- If the project has not been saved you will be prompted to save it, or

- You may a close project by closing all the open windows by clicking on the X in the tab,

Click here to close a project when one window remains open

- When the last project tab is closed the project will be closed and you will be prompted to save the project.

Copyright Eastwood Harris Pty Ltd 2020

42

EASTWOOD HARRIS PTY LTD.

Exiting Powerproject

- Select **File**, **Exi**t,
- Powerproject will ask you to save a project when you close a project, or shutdown the software without saving the project:

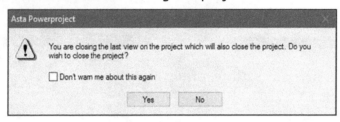

- The **File**, **Options**, **Edit** has an option to create a backup on saving a file and will be saved in the same directory with a *.bak extension,
- To open a *.BAK file just change the extension to *.PP.

43

EASTWOOD HARRIS PTY LTD.

Powerproject Help

- Powerproject help is all web based help is available by clicking on the Help button,
- UK support is through Elecosoft:
  Web: http://www.elecosoft.com/
  Tel: 01844 261609
  Email: support@elecosoft.com
- Australian support is available through Solid Support:
  Web: http://www.solidsupport.com.au/
  Tel: 02 9743 4666
  Email: helpdesk@solidsupport.com.au
- US support is available through Elecosoft LLC:
  Web: http://www.elecosoft.com/
  Tel: (855) 553-AST
  Email: inquiries@elecosoft.com

44

EASTWOOD HARRIS PTY LTD.

Workshop 1 – Creating a Project

- You will create a new project from a template,

- A project template in *.pp format titled Australian and US Powerproject Version 15 construction template has been loaded on the Eastwood Harris web site at www.eh.com.au Software Downloads page that has a number of the issues with the UK templates resolved, including the default currency and calendar holidays,

- If you are from a country that uses the Dollar then you should download this file, save it in the Powerproject template directory and use this file,

- **NOTE:** This file has the UK calendars removed and the default Currency set to Dollars and cents with a $ symbol,

- You are welcome to use any other template, but your screen may not look the same as the ones in screen shots.

45

EASTWOOD HARRIS PTY LTD.

2 - NAVIGATION AND SETTING OPTIONS

- This module covers Powerproject screen and some of the navigation commands,

- The Powerproject screen is composed of a number of areas,

  - **Toolbars** – Contains shortcut buttons to menu functions,

  - **Barchart** – Information on your project in graphic form,

  - **Spreadsheet** – Information on your project in table form,

  - **Project View** – A window enabling the assignment of resources, calendars and codes by click and dragging,

  - **Object Edit Toolbar** – Used to edit tasks and/or links in the Gantt Chart,

  - **Date zone** – Shows the dates over the Gantt Chart,

  - **Properties View** – Allows you to edit the properties of a selected object.

46

Create and Update an Unresourced Project Using Elecosoft (Asta) Powerproject Version 15.2

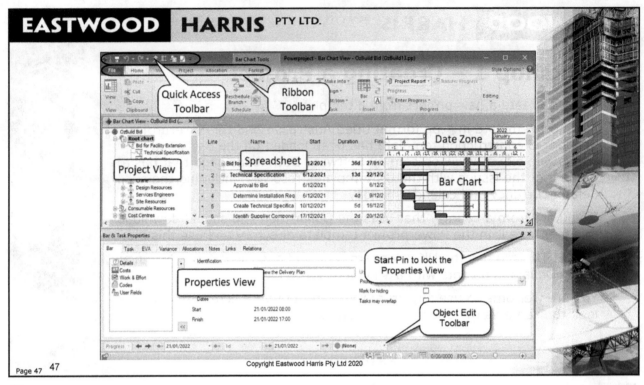

Screen Bands

- The default setting is with bands shown across the screen and applies to all projects on a computer:

- These bands may be removed, see next slide:

EASTWOOD HARRIS PTY LTD.

Removing Screen Bands

- To remove the thick coloured bands running across the screen,

- Select **File**, **Options**, **View** tab and uncheck Show sort bands in the bar chart,

- This is a system setting and applies to all projects you open.

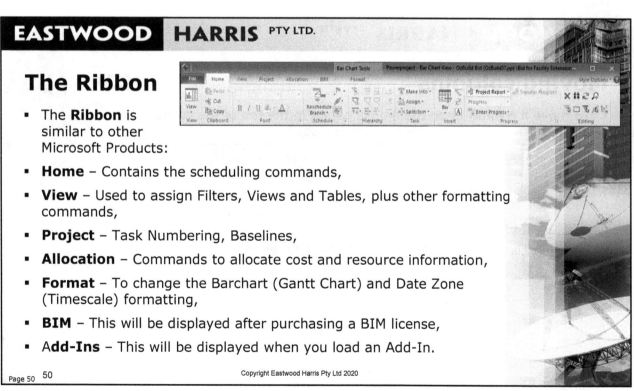

Uncheck **Show sort bands in the bar chart**

Page 49   49   Copyright Eastwood Harris Pty Ltd 2020

49

EASTWOOD HARRIS PTY LTD.

The Ribbon

- The **Ribbon** is similar to other Microsoft Products:

- **Home** – Contains the scheduling commands,

- **View** – Used to assign Filters, Views and Tables, plus other formatting commands,

- **Project** – Task Numbering, Baselines,

- **Allocation** – Commands to allocate cost and resource information,

- **Format** – To change the Barchart (Gantt Chart) and Date Zone (Timescale) formatting,

- **BIM** – This will be displayed after purchasing a BIM license,

- **Add-Ins** – This will be displayed when you load an Add-In.

Page 50   50   Copyright Eastwood Harris Pty Ltd 2020

50

EASTWOOD HARRIS PTY LTD.

Customizing the Toolbars

- The toolbars will not be covered in detail in this course as they operate the same way as all other Microsoft products,

- The **Ribbon Toolbar** has Tabs along the top and Ribbon Groups, which are groups of Command Buttons, below the Ribbon Tabs,

- Significant productivity improvements may be made by:

  - Moving the **Quick Access Toolbar** below the Ribbon Toolbar,

    - Ensuring that frequently used functions are made available on the Quick Access Toolbar,

      - **Minimize the Ribbon** which hides the Ribbon Toolbar until required,

- **NOTE:** You will import the Eastwood Harris Powerproject Quick Access toolbar in a workshop which is available from https://www.eh.com.au/software.html.

51

EASTWOOD HARRIS PTY LTD.

Moving columns

- To move a column place the mouse cursor in the top of the column title and it will turn into a double headed mouse,

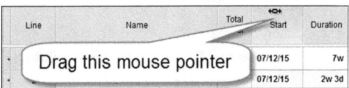

- Then left click and drag the column to the desired position.

52

24

EASTWOOD HARRIS PTY LTD.

Scaling the Date Zone

- Select a vertical line in the Date Zone,

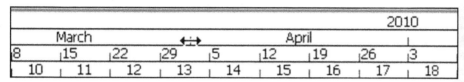

- Move the mouse in the Date Zone until a double headed arrow is displayed,
- Left click and drag it left or right to change the Date Zone scaling.

53

EASTWOOD HARRIS PTY LTD.

Moving the Date Zone

- Left click and hold in the Date Zone,

- A hand icon will be displayed in the Date Zone,
- Drag left or right to move the Date Zone left or right,
- You may also use the Scroll Bars at the bottom of the screen to move the Date Zone left and right.

54

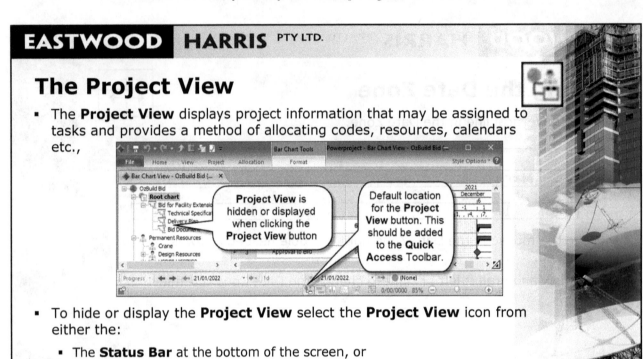

The Project View

- The **Project View** displays project information that may be assigned to tasks and provides a method of allocating codes, resources, calendars etc.,

- To hide or display the **Project View** select the **Project View** icon from either the:

    - The **Status Bar** at the bottom of the screen, or

    - You should add the icon to the **Quick Access Toolbar.**

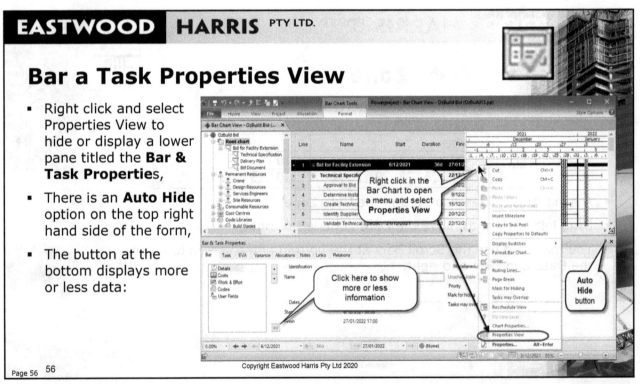

Bar a Task Properties View

- Right click and select Properties View to hide or display a lower pane titled the **Bar & Task Propertie**s,

- There is an **Auto Hide** option on the top right hand side of the form,

- The button at the bottom displays more or less data:

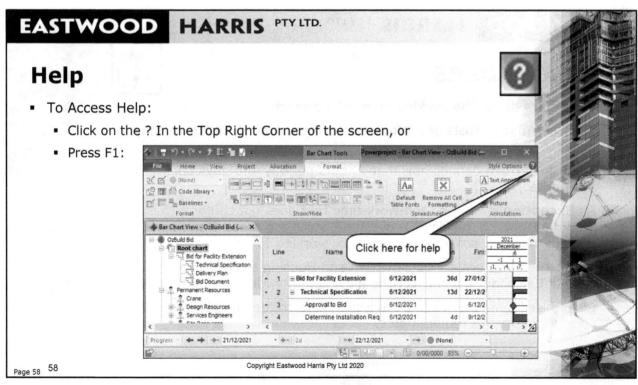

EASTWOOD HARRIS PTY LTD.

Workshop 2 – Navigation and Setting Your Project Options

- In this workshop you will:
    - Import the Eastwood Harris Quick Access Toolbar and
    - Practice navigating around the screen.

EASTWOOD HARRIS PTY LTD.

3 - CALENDARS

- **Calendars** define the working times of a project,
- The **Calendar** consists of a **Work Pattern** to which **Exceptions** may be added,
- A **Work Pattern** defines how many hours per day and days per week are worked,
- An **Exception** is work or non-work time that does not conform to the Work Pattern. E.g. holidays or overtime which are called **Non Work time** in many US software packages, or working Sundays,
- **Note:** The Powerproject Construction and Housing templates both contain Calendars which cover the most common UK working patterns,
- Customised templates should have calendars created and tailored to suit your organisation's requirements.

EASTWOOD HARRIS PTY LTD.

Work Pattern

- A calendar is constructed of two components found in the Library Explorer and one is the Work Patterns,

- They are given a name,

- Each day of the week is assigned the work start and finish times,

- Assigned Override Definitions that are used to define summary durations in weeks, months and years,

- These are not covered in this course as existing ones may be used.

Copyright Eastwood Harris Pty Ltd 2020

61

EASTWOOD HARRIS PTY LTD.

Exceptions

- A calendar is constructed of two components that are found in the **Library Explorer** and the second one is the **Exceptions**,

- These are given a name,

- Formatting, allowing different work or non work to be displayed on the Gantt Chart in different colours and

- Defines as Working time or Non-working time.

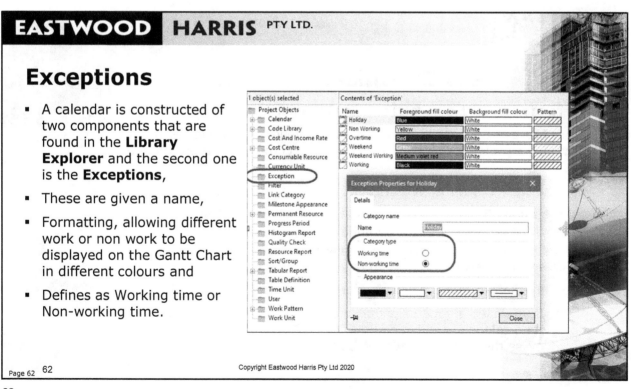

Copyright Eastwood Harris Pty Ltd 2020

62

29

EASTWOOD HARRIS PTY LTD.

Displaying available Calendars

- Calendars may be accessed from the Library Explorer or the Project View as per the picture below:

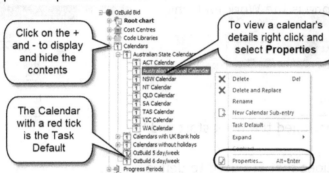

- The Task Default is the calendar assigned to new tasks and has a red tick in the Project View,

- Note: If no Task Default is set then no calendar will be assigned to new tasks and the schedule will not calculate properly.

EASTWOOD HARRIS PTY LTD.

Creating New Calendars

- There are several methods of creating calendars:

- From **Library Explorer** copy an existing calendar from another project or within a project using the copy and paste commands, then rename and edit,

- Use the **New Calendar Wizard**, which may be run from either:

  - The Library Explorer after selecting a Calendar Node and selecting New Calendar or New Calendar Sub-entry, or

  - The Project View after selecting a Calendar Node and selecting New Calendar or New Calendar Sub-entry,

- You may then edit your new calendar,

- Note: If you have a good calendar, then it is simpler to copy and paste an existing calendar and change the **Work Pattern** and **Exceptions** and not use the **New Calendar Wizard**.

Creating a new calendar using Library Explorer and the New Calendar Wizard:

- To create a new calendar open the **Library Explorer** and select the calendars folder,

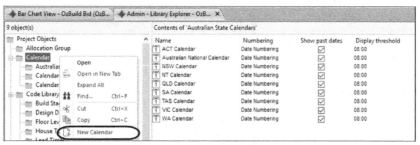

- Right click on Calendar and select **New Calendar** to run **the New Calendar Wizard**,

- A new calendar may also be created from the **Project View** by left clicking and selecting **New Calendar Sub-entry**.

Copyright Eastwood Harris Pty Ltd 2020

65

Copying an existing calendar

- This is often the simplest way to create a new calendar,

- Open **Library Explorer**,

- Left click on the Calendar folder in the left hand window,

- Right click on the calendar you want to copy,

- Select Copy,

- Select Paste, then rename,

- You may then edit the new calendar.

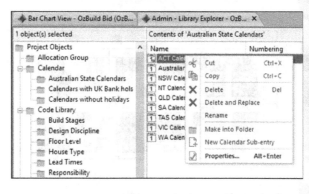

Copyright Eastwood Harris Pty Ltd 2020

66

Copying Exceptions between Calendars

- Once you have created your calendar you may wish to copy standard exceptions like Public Holidays from another calendar,

  - Open the calendar that has the exceptions you wish to Copy,
  - Right click on any date, and
  - Select Copy Exceptions to.

Copy Exceptions

Copy exceptions from:
- ● Selected dates only   ○ Entire calendar

Of these types:
- ☐ Holiday
- ☐ Non Working
- ☐ Overtime
- ☐ Weekend
- ☐ Working

To these calendars:
- ☐ 5 day week, UK Holiday
- ☐ 5 day week, UK Hols +
- ☐ 5.5 day week
- ☐ 5.5 day week, UK Holid
- ☐ 5.5 day week, UK Hols
- ☐ 6 day week
- ☐ 6 day week, UK Holiday
- ☐ 6 day week, UK Hols +

[Select All Types]   [Select All Calendars]

☑ Warn me about conflicting exception assignments

[Copy Exceptions]   [Cancel]

Half Day Exception

- Each day in the Calendar has a Work Pattern assigned to it,

- An Exception is any day which does not follow that Work Pattern,

- A half tone colour, e.g. pink instead of red, would be a half day exception.

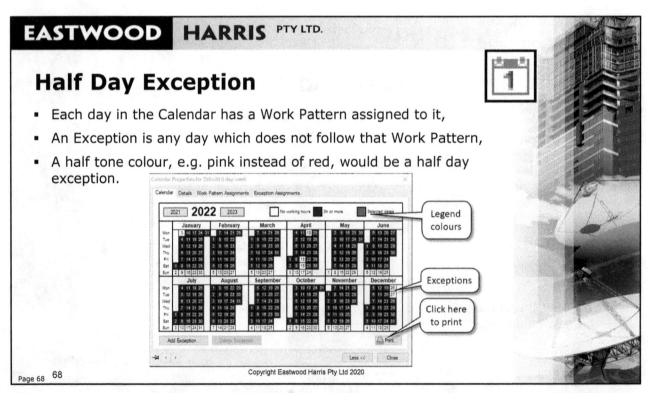

EASTWOOD HARRIS PTY LTD.

Viewing Working Hours

- Double click on any day to view the working hours:

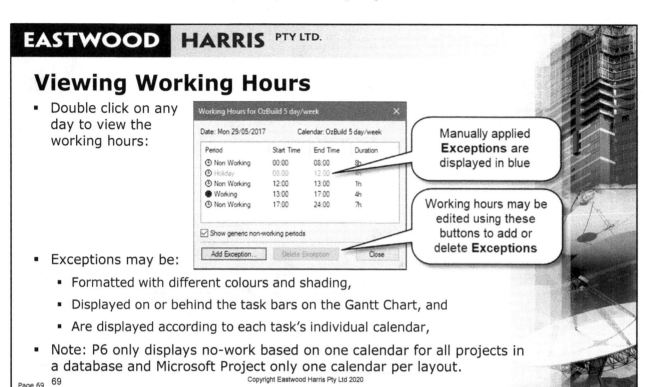

Working Hours for OzBuild 5 day/week

Date: Mon 29/05/2017   Calendar: OzBuild 5 day/week

Period	Start Time	End Time	Duration
⏱ Non Working	00:00	08:00	8h
⏱ Holiday	08:00	12:00	
⏱ Non Working	12:00	13:00	1h
⬤ Working	13:00	17:00	4h
⏱ Non Working	17:00	24:00	7h

☑ Show generic non-working periods

[Add Exception...] [Delete Exception] [Close]

*Manually applied **Exceptions** are displayed in blue*

*Working hours may be edited using these buttons to add or delete **Exceptions***

- Exceptions may be:
  - Formatted with different colours and shading,
  - Displayed on or behind the task bars on the Gantt Chart, and
  - Are displayed according to each task's individual calendar,
- Note: P6 only displays no-work based on one calendar for all projects in a database and Microsoft Project only one calendar per layout.

EASTWOOD HARRIS PTY LTD.

Adding Calendar Exceptions

- To change working days into holiday or weekends into working days in your calendar:
- Left click on one or more date(s), these will now be highlighted in blue,
- Right Click and select the Assign Exception,
- Select the type of exception, e.g. Holiday,
- Then either:
  - Enter Start and end times, or
  - Tick the boxes to apply the exception From work pattern periods for both morning and afternoon,
  - Note: This is the recommended method, as the format of calendar non-work time and work time is the same, or
  - Select 24 hour.

EASTWOOD HARRIS PTY LTD.

Deleting Calendar Exceptions

- Ctrl + Left click to select date(s),
- Click on Delete Exception button to delete both Morning and Afternoon Exceptions when applied,
- Click Yes when prompted:

Copyright Eastwood Harris Pty Ltd 2020

71

EASTWOOD HARRIS PTY LTD.

Task Default Calendar...

- The Task Default calendar is assigned to all new tasks,
- Changing the Task Default calendar will not change the calendar assigned to any existing tasks, only new tasks,
- If using the "Powerproject Construction Template" you will see that there are a number of calendars to cover 5, 6 or 7 working day calendars with and without public holidays, which are based on the UK practices,
- You may copy and paste in Library Explorer to make copy an existing calendar:
  - To create new calendar in a project and edit it to manage work on different working times, or
  - Copy a calendar from one project to another,
- You may create your own new calendar using the New Calendar Wizard.

Copyright Eastwood Harris Pty Ltd 2020

72

34

Task Default Calendar

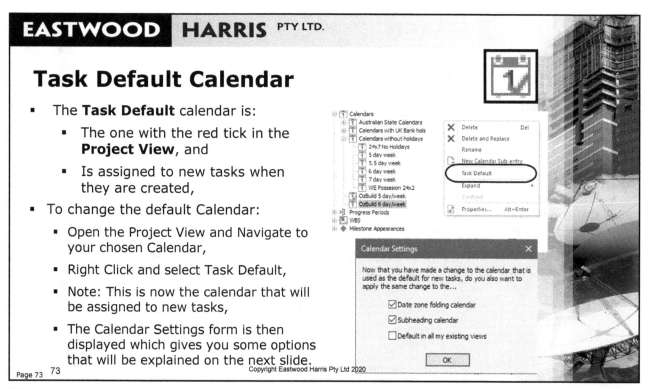

- The **Task Default** calendar is:
  - The one with the red tick in the **Project View**, and
  - Is assigned to new tasks when they are created,
- To change the default Calendar:
  - Open the Project View and Navigate to your chosen Calendar,
  - Right Click and select Task Default,
  - Note: This is now the calendar that will be assigned to new tasks,
  - The Calendar Settings form is then displayed which gives you some options that will be explained on the next slide.

73

Calendar Settings form

- Date zone folding calendar is the calendar used to hide non work time in the Gantt chart, covered in Formatting the Display section,
- Subheading calendar is explained in the picture below:

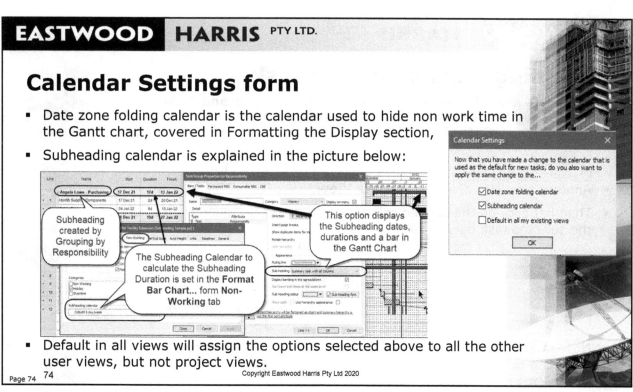

- Default in all views will assign the options selected above to all the other user views, but not project views.

74

EASTWOOD HARRIS PTY LTD.

Assigning a Calendar to a Task or Tasks

- The methods of assigning calendars to tasks are:
- The **Task Default** calendar is assigned when a task is created,
- One or more selected task/s may have their calendar changed by dragging a new calendar from the **Project View**,
- The **Calendar** column may be displayed or a table created with the **Calendar** column, then copy and paste may be used to assign a calendar to multiple tasks,
- The **Properties View** or the **Bar and Task Properties** form **Task**, **Dates** tab may be used to assign a calendar to a single task at a time.

Copyright Eastwood Harris Pty Ltd 2020

75

EASTWOOD HARRIS PTY LTD.

Assigning a Calendar to a task

- Calendars may be assigned to a single task in the **Bar and Task Properties** form or view, **Task**, **Dates** tab,

- Another way is to open the **Project View**,
- Then left click on the desired calendar, and drag the calendar on to one of the selected task bars:

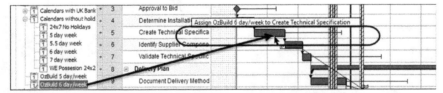

- **Note:** Select the Gantt Chart bars or the Line Number before dragging when assigning to multiple tasks.

Copyright Eastwood Harris Pty Ltd 2020

76

EASTWOOD HARRIS PTY LTD.

Assigning a Calendar to a task...

- When you apply a different Calendar to a task, the tasks duration and dates could change,

- You may control how you would like the task duration and finish date to be calculated by the new Calendar by selecting from the dialogue box that is displayed.

Change Task Calendar ✕

Changing the calendar can affect the start date, finish date and duration of a task. Please choose what you would like to happen:

◉ Retain the existing duration and change the dates if necessary

    The task will retain its existing duration. If the time units within the calendars differ (for example, if the working week is 5d in one calendar and 6d in another) or if the calendars have different holidays, the finish date of the task may be changed.

○ Retain the existing start and finish dates and change the duration if necessary

    The task will retain its existing start and finish dates where possible. If the time units or holidays within the calendars differ, the duration of the task may be changed. The dates may also be changed because of different holidays or time units.

○ Retain the absolute duration in terms of hours, minutes and seconds

    The absolute duration of the task will be retained. The formatted duration (for example 2w) may be changed, as may the start and finish dates because of different holidays or time units.

☐ Do not ask me again   OK

77

EASTWOOD HARRIS PTY LTD.

Assigning a Calendar to a task...

- The picture shows a task with a 5x8 calendar being assigned a 24x7 calendar with each of the three options:

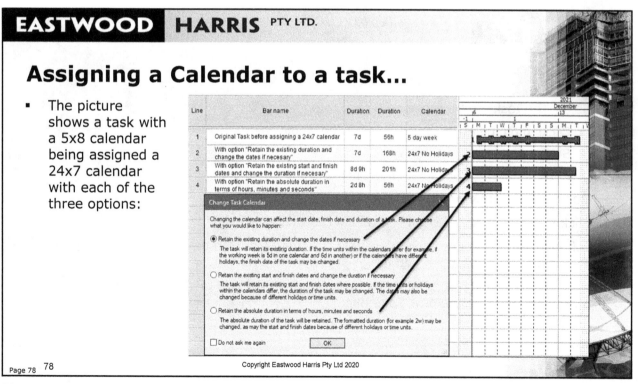

78

EASTWOOD HARRIS PTY LTD.

Assigning a Calendar to a task...

- You may be asked if you want to change the Date Zone Folding calendar:

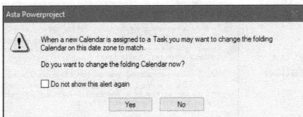

- The Date Zone Folding calendar controls what working time and non working time may be displayed or hidden from view on the Gantt Chart,

- For example Non work Time, Holidays or Weekends may be hidden,

- The project may need to be rescheduled to reflect any changes after a new calendar has been assigned.

Page 79   79   Copyright Eastwood Harris Pty Ltd 2020

79

EASTWOOD HARRIS PTY LTD.

Assigning a Calendar to multiple tasks

- Select the tasks to be assigned a new calendar by either:
  - Clicking on the row number to select the whole line, or
  - Selecting the bars in the Gantt Chart,
  - Note: the Gantt Charts bars must be highlighted,
- Open the Project View,
- Click the + next to Calendars to reveal the available Calendars,
- Left click on the desired calendar, hold the mouse button down and drag the Calendar on to a task and let go of the mouse button,
- Again you will be given choices as to how you would like to change your tasks as a result of the new Calendar.

Page 80   80   Copyright Eastwood Harris Pty Ltd 2020

80

EASTWOOD HARRIS PTY LTD.

Assigning a Calendar to the whole Project

- Select Ctrl A to select all activities,

- Open the Project View,

- Click the + next to Calendars to reveal the available Calendars,

- Left click on the desired calendar, hold the mouse button down and drag the Calendar on to a task and let go of the mouse button,

- Again you will be given choices as to how you would like to change your tasks as a result of the new Calendar.

Copyright Eastwood Harris Pty Ltd 2020

81

EASTWOOD **HARRIS** PTY LTD.

Formatting Exceptions Display on the Gantt Chart

- The display of Exception's Nonwork and Working time and colours is determined by the Format Bar Chart, Non-Working tab:

  - Non-working display necks the bars and must be unchecked to Draw Non-working shading On tasks,

  - Draw Non-working shading On tasks shades the Chart or Tasks,

  - Colours and patterns are set in the Library Explorer, Exception tab,

  - Categories selects what is shaded with the options above.

Copyright Eastwood Harris Pty Ltd 2020

82

EASTWOOD HARRIS PTY LTD.

Workshop 3 - Maintaining the Calendars

- We will create and edit two calendars for your project,
- You will create:
  - A 5 day per week calendar with some holidays by copying an exiting calendar and
  - A 6 day per week calendar by copying the 5 day per week calendar and edit it to create a new calendar with the same holidays.

83

EASTWOOD HARRIS PTY LTD.

4 - TASKS AND MILESTONES

In this module we will look at:
- Creating tasks
- Moving and editing tasks
- Creating milestones
- Understand the Difference between Bars and Tasks.

84

EASTWOOD HARRIS PTY LTD.

Creating tasks

- A task may be created by either:
  - Typing a name and duration into the column on the Spreadsheet, or
  - By using the cursor to draw onto the Bar Chart and then entering a name on the Spreadsheet,
- Once created, any task attribute may be edited using either the Spreadsheet or using the mouse on the task bar,
- Tasks may be added:
  - At the bottom of the list of tasks, or
  - By inserting a new task by right clicking and selecting Insert Bar, which inserts a task above the selected task, or
  - By inserting a new task by right clicking and selecting Insert Bar Below.

85

EASTWOOD **HARRIS** PTY LTD.

To Create tasks in the Spreadsheet

- Select the duration column for the first blank task,
- Enter the duration,
- Press Enter,
- A task is displayed on the Bar Chart,
- Enter the Name.

Line	Name	Start	Duration	Finish	May 20 · 27 135 · 136 · 137
1	First Task Name	20/05/19	3d	22/05/19	1

86

EASTWOOD HARRIS PTY LTD.

To create tasks on the Bar Chart

- Click the mouse on the Bar Chart on a line for the next task, the cursor will now be a cross,

- Left click and drag the mouse to the right,

Line	Name	Start	Duration	Finish	May		
					20	27	
1	First Task Name	20/05/19	3d	22/05/19	Start 23/05/19 Finish 27/05/19 Duration 3d		137

- The pop up box displays the task duration,

- The task name may be typed in before or after the task is created in the Gantt Chart.

EASTWOOD HARRIS PTY LTD.

Sorting and the Task Order

- As tasks are added they adopt the Natural Order,

- When a user double clicks on a task column header the tasks are sorted in ascending and then descending in the order of the column values,

- This often happens by accident and to bring the tasks back to the Natural Order you should select View, View data, Natural Order:

EASTWOOD HARRIS PTY LTD.

Moving and editing tasks

- Tasks may be moved and edited using either the mouse or the Object Edit Toolbar,
- Edit the Task Duration by editing the start or end date,
- Edit the Task Dates by simply moving the task to another position on the Gantt Chart,
- If your Reschedule Options is set to Auto reschedule then the task may just move back to the original start date location.

EASTWOOD HARRIS PTY LTD.

Using the mouse to adjust durations and dates:

- Tasks may be edited using either the mouse by placing the mouse at either end of the task or in the middle:

  - Placed in the middle adjusts the position of the task,

  - Placed at the start adjusts the Start Date, and changes the duration,

  - Placed at the end adjusts the End Date, and changes the duration,

- **NOTE:** When the Reschedule Options are set to Move to ASAP/ALAP and Auto reschedule then then this will schedule tasks and these commands will only adjust the durations of the tasks.

EASTWOOD HARRIS PTY LTD.

Moving bars vertically

- Moving bars vertically allows you to change the order of tasks within the project,

- Left click on the line number for the task you want to move. This selects the entire bar of information on both the Spreadsheet data and task on the Bar Chart,

Line	Name	Duration	Start	Finish	Total float	Free float	
1	Approval to Bid		06 Dec 21	06 Dec 21	8d	8d	
2	Determine Installation Requirements	4d	06 Dec 21	09 Dec 21	4d	4d	
3	Create Technical Specification	5d	06 Dec 21	10 Dec 21	3d	3d	
4	Identify Supplier Components	2d	06 Dec 21	07 Dec 21	6d	6d	

- Place the cursor over the task bar until the cursor is displayed shown in the picture above,

- Click and drag the bar to the new line above,

- Note: An applied View with a sort order may prevent this action.

93

EASTWOOD HARRIS PTY LTD.

Inserting bars

- To insert a new bar above a task:

  - Left click on the line number below where you want to insert your new line, Right click and select Insert Bar,

Line	Name	Duration	Start	Finish	Total float	Free float	
1	Approval to Bid		06 Dec 21	06 Dec 21	8d	8d	
2	Determine Installation Requirements	4d	06 Dec 21	09 Dec 21	4d	4d	
	Cut Ctrl+X	5d	06 Dec 21	10 Dec 21	3d	3d	
	Copy Ctrl+C						
	Paste Ctrl+V	2d	06 Dec 21	07 Dec 21	6d	6d	
	Paste Values	2d	06 Dec 21	07 Dec 21	6d	6d	
	Paste and Retain Links						
	Insert Bar Ins	4d	06 Dec 21	09 Dec 21	4d	4d	
	Insert Bar Below	8d	06 Dec 21	15 Dec 21	0d	0d	
	Delete Del	3d	06 Dec 21	08 Dec 21	6d	6d	

- To insert a new bar below a task:

  - Left click on the line number below where you want to insert your new line, Right click and select Insert Bar Below.

94

Understanding Milestones

- There are 2 types of Powerproject milestones, Start and Finish,

- Powerproject milestones calculate in a similar way to P6 milestones but display both Start and Finish Dates. Microsoft Project Milestones always calculate as a Powerproject Finish Milestone:

  - A Start Milestone will appear at the start of the next available work period, usually at the same time as the successor,

  - A Finish Milestone will appear at the end of the current work period, usually at the same time as the predecessor,

- E.g. if a predecessor task is completed on Friday afternoon,

  - A successor Finish Milestone will appear at the end of Friday afternoon,

  - A successor Start Milestone will appear on Monday morning,

- A Start Milestone is created by default.

Creating a Start Milestone

- To create a Start Milestone either,

  - Type in the Milestone name in a blank line and

  - Enter 0 in the duration column,

Line	Name	Duration	Start	Finish	Total float	Free float
1	Approval to Bid		06 Dec 21	06 Dec 21	8d	8d
2	Determine Installation Requirements	4d	06 Dec 21	09 Dec 21	4d	4d
3	Create Technical Specification	5d	06 Dec 21	10 Dec 21	3d	3d

- Or, go to the first blank line at the bottom of the screen in the Gantt Chart,

  - Right click and select Insert Milestone and

  - Type in the Milestone name:

- Note: The 0 Duration may not be displayed when the default is to display zeros as blank in the Table Definition Properties form.

EASTWOOD HARRIS PTY LTD.

To change a Start Milestone into a Finish Milestone:

- Right click on the Milestone icon in the Gantt Chart and select Make into – Finish Milestone:

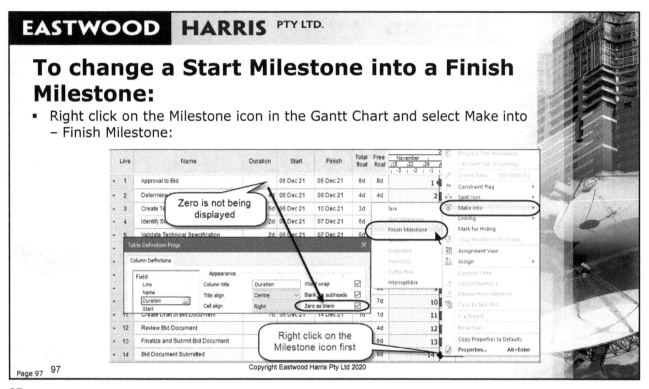

Copyright Eastwood Harris Pty Ltd 2020

97

EASTWOOD HARRIS PTY LTD.

Workshop 4 - Adding Tasks

- In this workshop you will add the project tasks,

- It is simpler to teach Powerproject by showing how you to enter the tasks first and then creating the summary tasks to represent the WBS Nodes which also called Products or Deliverables,

- Once a user understands the processes then the tasks and summary tasks may be entered in any order.

Copyright Eastwood Harris Pty Ltd 2020

98

EASTWOOD HARRIS PTY LTD.

5 - SUMMARY TASKS

This module will cover the following topics:

- Understanding Summary Tasks,
- Creating Summary tasks,
- Summarising tasks,
- Adding and removing tasks from Summary Tasks,
- Removing Summary Tasks,
- Formatting Summary Tasks and
- Navigating a program using the Project View and Summary Tasks.

Copyright Eastwood Harris Pty Ltd 2020

EASTWOOD HARRIS PTY LTD.

Understanding Summary Tasks

- Summary Tasks are used to summarize and group tasks under a hierarchy of Parent or Summary Tasks,
- They are used to present different views of your project during planning, scheduling and updating,
- These headings are normally based on your project WBS,
- Summary Tasks may be used to represent one or more of the following:
  - Work Breakdown Structure
  - The project phases and stages
  - Areas, floor or physical locations
  - Trades of disciplines
  - Systems and sub-systems
- **Note:** Summary Tasks calculate in a similar way to Microsoft Project Summary Tasks and P6 WBS activities.

Copyright Eastwood Harris Pty Ltd 2020

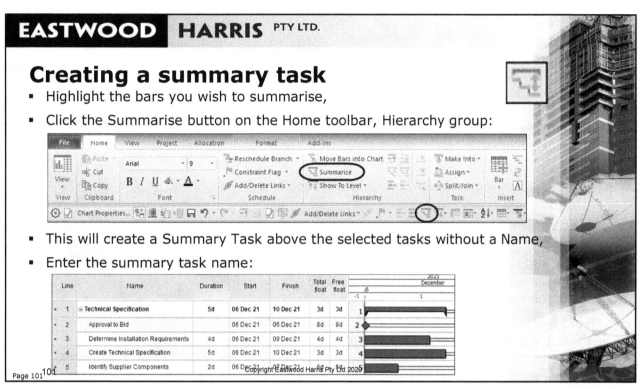

Creating a summary task

- Highlight the bars you wish to summarise,

- Click the Summarise button on the Home toolbar, Hierarchy group:

- This will create a Summary Task above the selected tasks without a Name,

- Enter the summary task name:

Line	Name	Duration	Start	Finish	Total float	Free float	December 2021
1	⊟ Technical Specification	5d	06 Dec 21	10 Dec 21	3d	3d	
2	Approval to Bid		06 Dec 21	06 Dec 21	8d	8d	
3	Determine Installation Requirements	4d	06 Dec 21	09 Dec 21	4d	4d	
4	Create Technical Specification	5d	06 Dec 21	10 Dec 21	3d	3d	
5	Identify Supplier Components	2d	06 Dec 21	07 Dec 21			

Page 101

Copyright Eastwood Harris Pty Ltd 2020

101

Rolling up and opening summary tasks

- Highlight the Summary Task bar in the Gantt Chart so the ◄▯► pointer is displayed and double click,

- Double click again to display the tasks,

- The **Show To Level button** may also be used to summarise tasks to Levels:

- Clicking on the + and – to the left of the Task Name, as with Microsoft Project,

- **Note:** The **Show To Level button** function will only operate to Level 1 and All Levels when the tasks are grouped by codes.

Line	Name	Duration	Start	Finish	Total float	Free float	
1	⊟ Bid for Facility Extension	8d	06 Dec 21	15 Dec 21	0d	0d	OzBuild
2	⊞ Technical Specification	5d	06 Dec 21	10 Dec 21	3d	3d	OzBuild
3	⊞ Delivery Plan	8d	06 Dec 21	15 Dec 21	0d	0d	OzBuild
4	⊞ Bid Document	6d	06 Dec 21	13 Dec 21	2d	2d	OzBuild 5 day/week

Page 102

Copyright Eastwood Harris Pty Ltd 2020

102

EASTWOOD HARRIS PTY LTD.

Adding & Removing Tasks from Summary Task

- Select the task or tasks by clicking on the line number to select the bar(s),

- To add a task to a Summary Task click on the Indent button on the Home toolbar, Hierarchy group:

- Bars are added to the summary that is above the selected task or tasks,

- To remove a task from a Summary Task click on the Outdent button on the Home toolbar, Hierarchy group, which will outdent the task or tasks so they are no longer under the summary task,

- **Note:** Unlike Microsoft Project, outdenting all tasks under a Summary Task in Powerproject will delete the Summary Task.

Copyright Eastwood Harris Pty Ltd 2020

EASTWOOD HARRIS PTY LTD.

Deleting Summary Tasks

To delete a Summary Task either:

- Select all the tasks under a Summary Task,

- Click the Outdent button from the **Home** toolbar, **Hierarchy** group,

- The Summary Task will be deleted after the last Task has been Outdented,

Or:

- Delete the Summary Task which will also delete all of the Detailed Tasks underneath,

NOTE: Deleting all Detailed Tasks under a Summary Task will not delete a Summary Task and you will end up with a Summary Task with no Detailed Tasks under it.

Copyright Eastwood Harris Pty Ltd 2020

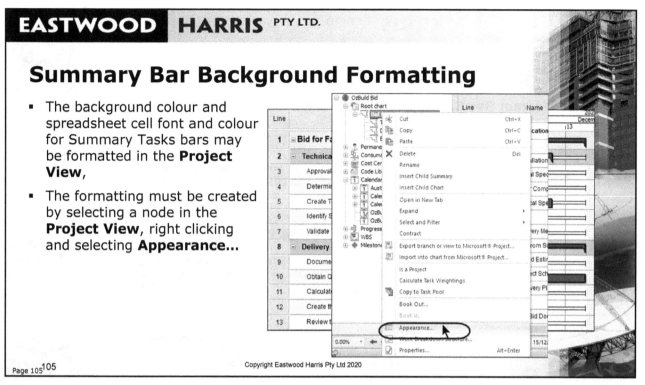

Copyright Eastwood Harris Pty Ltd 2020

105

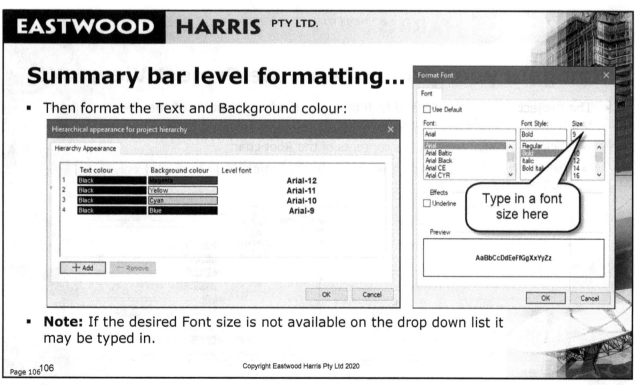

- **Note:** If the desired Font size is not available on the drop down list it may be typed in.

Copyright Eastwood Harris Pty Ltd 2020

106

51

Summary bar level formatting

- Select **Format Bar Chart, General** tab and choose Use summary row colouring on:

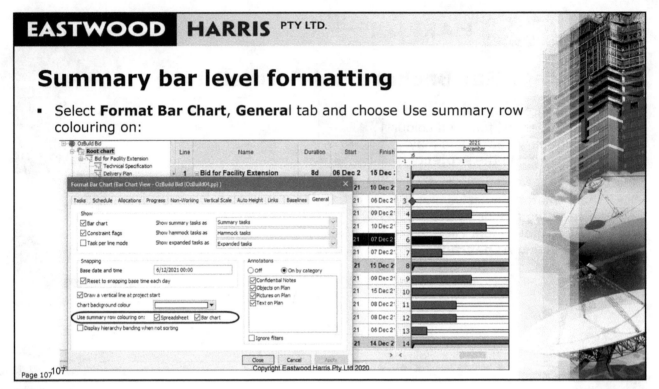

Page 107

107

Navigate your project with the Project View

- The Project View may be used to filter on non adjacent parts of the program and display the tasks associated with the selected nodes:

  - Click the '+' sign to open the contents of the Root chart,

  - Ctrl + Left click on some summary bars in the Project View to display only the tasks associated with the selected nodes:

Page 108

108

EASTWOOD HARRIS PTY LTD.

Workshop 5 - Entering Summary Tasks

In this workshop you will create some Summary Tasks.

- A Summary Task at Level 1 for Phase entitled **Bid for Facility Extension** and

- A Summary at Level 2 for each of the three Products the project is delivering:

  - Technical Specification

  - Delivery Plan

  - Bid Document

109

EASTWOOD HARRIS PTY LTD.

6 - LINKING TASKS TO CREATE A CRITICAL PATH SCHEDULE

- This module will cover how to link tasks to create a critical path program,

- The predecessor is the task at the start of the link and the successor is the task at the end of the link,

- The predecessor controls the start or finish of the successor,

- When there are multiple links between two tasks then the driving predecessor/s control/s the start or finish of the successor,

- Link Categories may be assigned to links so they may formatted or made inactive, in turn allowing multiple logic options in one program,

- Links may also be assigned Notes.

110

EASTWOOD HARRIS PTY LTD.

Understanding Leads and Lags in Powerproject

- MSP and P6 calculate the lead or lag on the link, thus the link is assigned the lead or lag, but

- Powerproject calculates the leads and lags on the predecessor and/or successor tasks,

- A Powerproject lead or lag is specified from the start or finish of the predecessor or successor in duration or percent of the task duration, thus allowing:

  - An unlimited number of links between tasks,

  - The lag calendar to be either the predecessor's or successor's or both and

  - Partial Critical Paths calculated through tasks.

Copyright Eastwood Harris Pty Ltd 2020

111

EASTWOOD HARRIS PTY LTD.

Preparing to Link Tasks using the Root Chart

- Often it is better to reduce the number of tasks in view by selecting the appropriate nodes in the Root Chart,

- This function may only be used when tasks are grouped under Summary Tasks, but may not be used when tasks are grouped by codes or other attributes,

- The picture below shows only the tasks under the two selected Summary tasks:

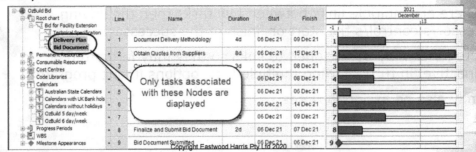

Copyright Eastwood Harris Pty Ltd 2020

112

EASTWOOD HARRIS PTY LTD.

Preparing to Link Tasks using Zoom Slider

- To make it simpler to assign Link consider using the **Zoom Slider** before adding Links to enlarge the task bars,

- Unlike Microsoft Project this function does not mess up your **Date Zone** formatting.

EASTWOOD HARRIS PTY LTD.

Link types

- There are 4 types of links as in other software:

  - **Finish to Start**, or often called a **Normal** link,

  - **Start to Start**

  - **Finish to Finish**

  - **Start to Finish**, which is illogical as the successor is before the predecessor,

- The predecessor controls the start or finish of the successor,

- The direction of the arrow goes from the predecessor to successor and

- Links may also be drawn starting and ending anywhere along the length of a predecessor or successor which creates a **Lead** or **Lag**.

Creating Links

There are many ways to create links:

- Drawing with the mouse, which is the most natural method and may be used to assign Leads and Lags,

- Select the tasks and use the **Block Linking** function,

- **Note:** Block Linking only links from top to bottom and not in the order that tasks are selected like P6 and MSP,

- Using the **Link From/To** form, which may be opened in a number of ways including:

  - **Bar and Task Properties** form or view,

  - From a Predecessor or Successor column,

    - Then the **Line Numbers** may be typed in or

    - The **Link From/To** form opened,

  - Gant chart menu.

Page 115¹¹⁵

115

Drawing Links...

- Links are drawn between tasks using the following cursor shapes:

  - End link
    Linking from the end of a task

  - Start Link
    Linking from the start of a task

  - Mid Link
    Linking from the middle of a task

  - Note: The No Entry sign indicates that the mouse in not in a position to create a link and releasing the mouse will open the Link From/To form.

Page 116¹¹⁶

116

EASTWOOD HARRIS PTY LTD.

Drawing a Finish to Start link

- To draw a Finish to Start link between 2 tasks:
  - Place the mouse at the end and at the top or bottom corner of the (predecessor) to display the end link cursor,
  - Left click & drag to draw the link to the start of the corresponding (successor) task to display the end link cursor,
  - Release the mouse when the start link cursor is displayed,
- A link is made between the 2 tasks,
- The link arrow is green which indicates the link is selected,
- Click elsewhere on the barchart to deselect the link.

Page 117¹¹⁷   Copyright Eastwood Harris Pty Ltd 2020

117

EASTWOOD HARRIS PTY LTD.

Drawing other links without lag

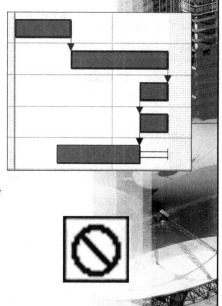

- To draw:
  - Start to Start links, or
  - Finish to Finish links, or
  - Start to Finish links,
- Place the mouse at the start or end and at the top or bottom corner of the first (predecessor) and displaying the start or end link cursor,
- Left click & drag to draw the link to the start or finish of the corresponding (successor) task,
- Dragging into a blank area will display a **No Entry** sign and releasing the mouse will open the **Link From/To** form and link information may be manually entered.

Page 118¹¹⁸   Copyright Eastwood Harris Pty Ltd 2020

118

EASTWOOD HARRIS PTY LTD.

Drawing Mid Links...

- Leads are called Negative Lags in products such as Microsoft Project and P6,

- This document will use the term Leads,

- In Powerproject a Lead or Lag is assigned to the task and not the link,

- A predecessor and a successor may both be assigned a Lead or Lag,

- A **Mid Link** is created when either the predecessor or successor or both have a Lead or Lag,

- A link may be drawn from the middle of the predecessor and/or to middle of a successor to create a **Mid Link**,

- Thus in Powerproject the Lead or Lag is assigned to the tasks and not on the Link as in P6 or MSP.

EASTWOOD HARRIS PTY LTD.

Drawing a Mid Link

To draw a **Mid Link**:

- Place the cursor in the middle of the task so that the **Mid Link** cursor is displayed,

- A pop up box will indicate where during the task you are linking from, i.e. the Lead or Lag that you are assigning,

  - A positive value is a Lag from the start,

  - A negative value is a Lead from the end,

- Left click at the desired position and drag the pointer to the desired position on the successor task,

- Release the mouse when the corresponding link cursor is displayed,

- Double Click on the link to open the **Link Properties** form to review the link details.

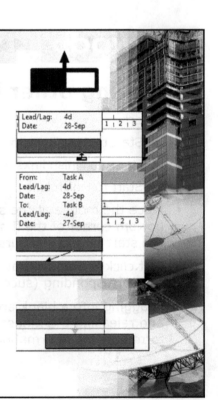

Drawing Mid Links with a Predecessor Lag

- When a predecessor **Mid Link** is drawn there are two options for the position of the predecessor **Mid Link**, it may be calculated from:

  - A distance from the start of the predecessor, or

  - A distance from the predecessor's nearest end point,

- When the mouse is placed over the middle of a predecessor **Mid Link** is calculated from the:

  - Start of the predecessor task plus a Lag,

- When the mouse is placed over the middle of a predecessor and the **Crtl** key is pressed then the **Mid Link** is calculated from the nearest end point and is be calculated either from the:

  - Start of the predecessor task plus a Lag, or

  - A Lead (Negative Lag) from the end of the predecessor task, as per the lower picture.

Lag calculated from start of task

| Lead/Lag: | 4d |
| Date: | 28-Sep |

Lead calculated from end of task

| Lead/Lag: | -2d |
| Date: | 28-Sep-18 |

Page 121 121   Copyright Eastwood Harris Pty Ltd 2020

121

Drawing Mid Links with a Successor Lag

- There are two options for the position of the successor **Mid Link** when a **Mid Link** is drawn to a successor, it may be calculated from:

  - A distance from the end of the successor, or

  - A distance from the successor's nearest end point,

- When the mouse is drawn to the middle of a successor the Mid Link is calculated by the:

  - Finish of the successor less a Lead,

- When the mouse is drawn to the middle of a successor and the Crtl key is pressed then the **Mid Link** is calculated from the nearest end from the:

  - Finish of the successor less a Lead, or

  - Start of the successor task plus a Lag, see the second picture.

From:	Task A
Lead/Lag:	0d
Date:	30-Sep
To:	Task B
Lead/Lag:	-2d
Date:	29-Sep

From:	Task A
Lead/Lag:	0d
Date:	30-Sep-18
To:	Task B
Lead/Lag:	2d
Date:	26-Sep-18

Page 122 122   Copyright Eastwood Harris Pty Ltd 2020

122

EASTWOOD HARRIS PTY LTD.

Drawing Mid Links with Predecessor and Successor Lead or Lag

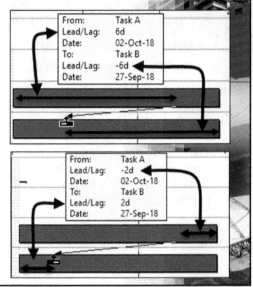

- When a **Mid Link** is drawn from the middle of a predecessor to the middle of a successor, there are two options for the calculation of the position of the successor **Mid Link**, it may be calculated from:

  - The start of the predecessor plus a Lag to the end of the successor less a Lead,

  - In the picture the predecessor Lag is 6d and successor Lead is -6d, or

  - When the **Ctrl** key is held down then it is drawn from nearest end of the predecessor task to the nearest end of the successor task,

  - In the second picture the predecessor Lead is -2d and successor Lag is 2d.

123

EASTWOOD HARRIS PTY LTD.

Drawing Mid Links - Summary

124

Displaying the Lead/Lag Popup box

- To ensure the **Lead/Lag popup** box displayed you need to open the **File**, **Options**, **General** tab, and

- Check the **Show Lead/Lag popup**,

- This makes it easier to see the lag *being added:*

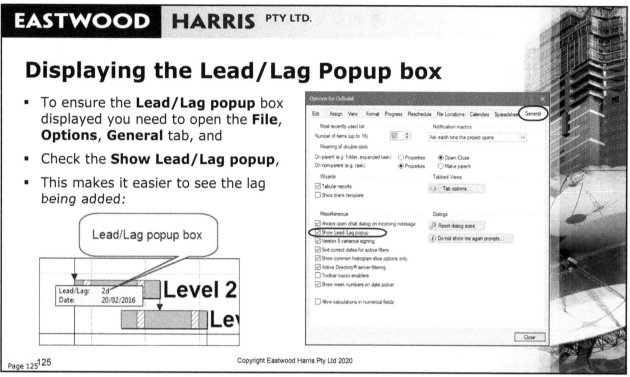

125

Drawing links with a FS + Lag...

- To create a link with a:

    - Finish to Start with a Lag on the predecessor, or

    - Finish to Finish with a Lag on the predecessor, or

    - Joining to any point on the successor,

- Place the cursor at the predecessor task bottom right hand corner, when link icon appears, press and hold the **Shift** key,

- Left click and hold the left mouse key down,

- Keep holding the right mouse button and drag the cursor right horizontally,

Continues on next slide...

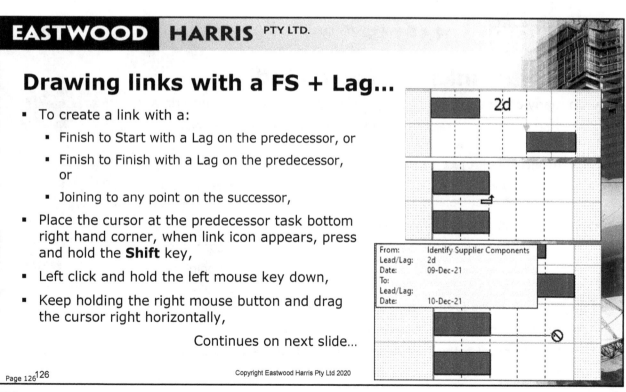

126

Drawing links with a FS + Lag

- Once you have reached the required lag RELEASE THE SHIFT KEY but keep hold of your mouse button,

- Drag to the successor and select the point at which you wish to link too on the successor and release the mouse,

- **Note:** This is often considered bad practice as it represents a missing task, but this demonstrates how the software operates.

Page 127 127

127

How Mid Links are Calculated

- In many other software packages like Microsoft Project and Primavera P6:

  - The lead or lag is calculated on the link and is assigned a calendar for all tasks in one project,

  - In Microsoft Project the successor calendar is used, and

  - In Primavera P6 there is a choice of 4 calendars, predecessor, successor, 24 hour or Project Default,

- Powerproject has more flexibility and a lead or lag:

  - May be put on either or both the predecessor or successor tasks,

  - A lead or lag may be placed at a duration from the start point or end point of both the predecessor and successor,

  - The lead or lag is calculated on the respective task calendar,

  - Multiple Mid Links are allowed between two tasks,

  - Partial Critical paths may be calculated for tasks with more than one link between them.

Page 128 128

128

Linking tasks from the Gantt Chart Right click menu

- To link multiple tasks from the Gantt Chart right click menu or clicking on a tool bar **Add Link** icon:
  - Select the task or tasks to be linked,
  - Right click in the Gantt Chart,
  - Select **Linking**, **Add Link...**, or
  - Click on the **Add Link** tool bar icon,
  - The **Link From/To** form will be displayed,
  - A this point there are some options explained on the next slide.

Copyright Eastwood Harris Pty Ltd 2020

129

Linking tasks from the Gantt Chart left click menu

One option is:

- Select either the **Link to selected** or **Link from selected** option,

- Complete the rest of the criteria by typing in the boxes underneath Link the selected items meeting the following criteria,

- **Note:** there is no lookup in these fields,

- When you click on **Link** there is no confirmation and it is difficult to see the result.

Copyright Eastwood Harris Pty Ltd 2020

130

63

EASTWOOD **HARRIS** PTY LTD.

Linking tasks from the Gantt Chart left click menu

Another option is to:

- Select the **Link Type**,

- Then click on **Limit linking to items in the following scope**,

- Select a Summary task that holds the task/s you wish to create a link too,

- Click on the Link button and you will be presented with a list of tasks under the selected summary task,

- Select one or more to create a link to your task and click **OK**.

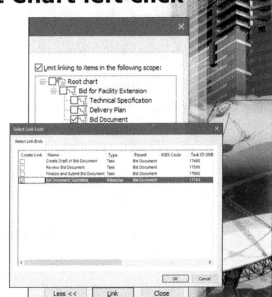

Page 131 131   Copyright Eastwood Harris Pty Ltd 2020

131

EASTWOOD **HARRIS** PTY LTD.

Dragging into a blank area to open the Link From/To form

- The **Link From/To** form may be displayed when you draw a link into a blank area of the Bar Chart and proceed as outlined in earlier slides:

Page 132 132   Copyright Eastwood Harris Pty Ltd 2020

132

EASTWOOD HARRIS PTY LTD.

Linking

- Two or more non consecutive tasks may be linked using the Linking function,

- Select non adjacent tasks to be linked by Ctl clicking on the Gantt Chart bar or **Line Number**, not the **Task Name**, or

- Click and drag on tasks that are next to each other,

- Click on the **Link** tasks toolbar button and the tasks will be linked with a Finish to Start link,

- **Note:** This function ignores the order that the tasks are selected in and only links from top to bottom for the selected tasks. P6 and Microsoft Project link in the order they were selected.

133

EASTWOOD **HARRIS** PTY LTD.

Link Task Mode

- This function is enabled by clicking on the **Link Task Mode** icon or **Ctl+F3**, which is probably simpler,

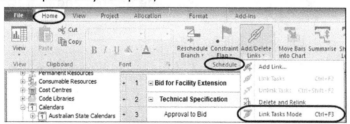

- Tasks will be linked with a **Finish - Start** link as they are clicked with the mouse,

- The user then has to turn off the function by clicking on the **Link Task Mode** icon or **Ctl+F3** before using other functions.

A chain icon will appear when the function is on

134

65

EASTWOOD HARRIS PTY LTD.

Editing and Deleting Links

- A selected link is green and may be deleted by pressing the **Delete** key or using the **Unlink Task** button,

- Links may be edited in the **Link Properties** form which may be opened by:

  - Selecting the link and then right clicking and selecting Properties,

  - Opening the **Bar and Task Properties** form or view,

  - Clicking in a **Predecessor** or **Successor** column cell,

  - Successor Links may be reassigned to another task by dragging, see next slide,

- To deselect a link, click elsewhere in the Bar Chart.

Copyright Eastwood Harris Pty Ltd 2020

135

EASTWOOD HARRIS PTY LTD.

Moving Successor Links

- When a link has the incorrect successor it may be 'dragged' with the mouse to the correct task and does not need to be deleted and redrawn, as with P6 and Microsoft project,

  - Click on the link to select it and it will go green,

  - Hover the cursor over the end of the link you wish the move until a 'cross' cursor becomes visible,

  - The link successor may be dragged to the correct successor.

Copyright Eastwood Harris Pty Ltd 2020

136

EASTWOOD HARRIS PTY LTD.

Reviewing Logic using Tables

- Logic may be reviewed in Tables with predecessor and/or successor columns

- Powerproject has many more option in the **Table Definition** form than other products for reviewing link information in columns,

- This includes the task **Name** or **ID** or **Line Number** and **Lead** and **Lag** details by selecting **All Details** or **Link Notes** or **Link Category**.

137

EASTWOOD HARRIS PTY LTD.

Percent Lead and Lag

- Double clicking on a Link will open the **Link Properties** form where Links may be edited,

- One interesting function of Powerproject is the ability to enter a **Percent lag**, which is available in MSP but not P6,

- Thus the Lead or Lag duration changes in proportion to the Task Duration,

- **Note:** If all leads and lags are entered as a Percentage this may allow a **Monte Carlo** evaluation to be performed on a schedule.

138

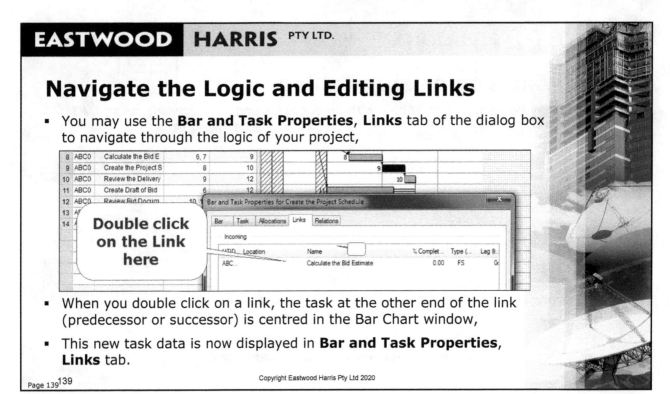

Navigate the Logic and Editing Links

- You may use the **Bar and Task Properties**, **Links** tab of the dialog box to navigate through the logic of your project,

- When you double click on a link, the task at the other end of the link (predecessor or successor) is centred in the Bar Chart window,

- This new task data is now displayed in **Bar and Task Properties**, **Links** tab.

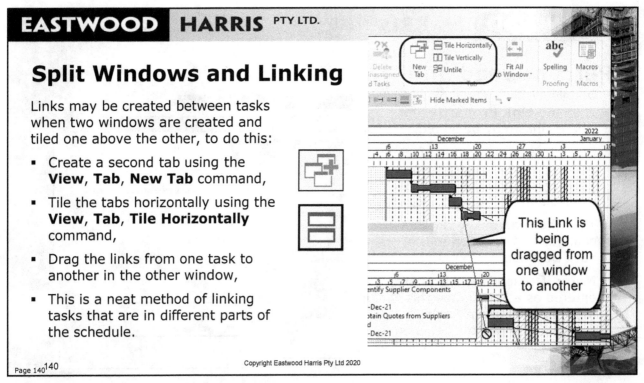

Split Windows and Linking

Links may be created between tasks when two windows are created and tiled one above the other, to do this:

- Create a second tab using the **View**, **Tab**, **New Tab** command,

- Tile the tabs horizontally using the **View**, **Tab**, **Tile Horizontally** command,

- Drag the links from one task to another in the other window,

- This is a neat method of linking tasks that are in different parts of the schedule.

Reviewing Logic using the Network Viewer

- The **Network Viewer** is used to review the logic and other project data,

- This is often referred to as a **Network Diagram** or a **PERT** diagram,

- The button to view the **Network** is found on the **Ribbon** toolbar under **Project**, **Data**.

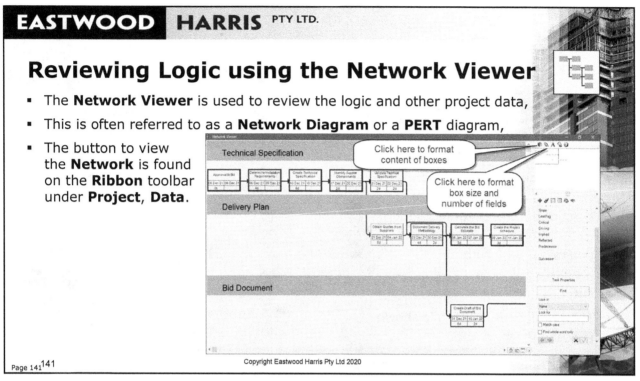

Reschedule

- When you have linked your tasks you may **Reschedule** the project,

- If you have **Reschedule** set to **Automatic** under the **Reschedule Options** then you will not need to reschedule,

- The **Reschedule** option performs a series of **Critical Path** calculations:

  - Calculates the **Early Dates**,
  - Calculates the **Late Dates**,
  - Calculates **Total Float**,
  - Calculates **Free Float**,
  - Calculates the earliest project end date.

To Reschedule the Whole Project:

- If you do not have **Automatic schedule** set and after making changes one would normally **Reschedule** the whole project,

- To **Reschedule** the whole project:
  - Click the **Reschedule All** tool bar button, or
  - Press the **F9** button,

- Accept the defaults, and press **OK**,

- The project critical path is shown outlined in red.

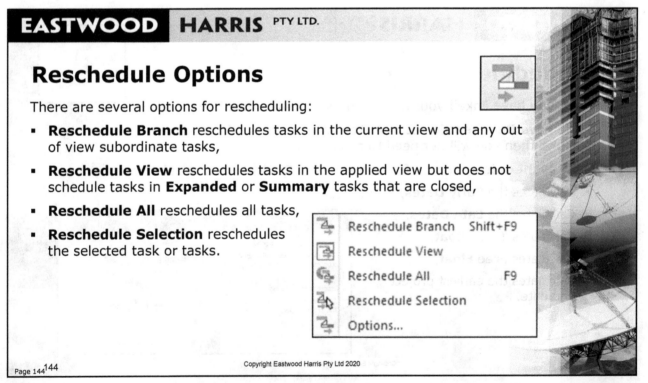

Reschedule Options

There are several options for rescheduling:

- **Reschedule Branch** reschedules tasks in the current view and any out of view subordinate tasks,

- **Reschedule View** reschedules tasks in the applied view but does not schedule tasks in **Expanded** or **Summary** tasks that are closed,

- **Reschedule All** reschedules all tasks,

- **Reschedule Selection** reschedules the selected task or tasks.

Understanding the File, Options, Reschedule form

- The **File, Options, Reschedule** form has some features not seen in other software, which we will not cover in this course,

- The **Auto reschedule** section allows manual or automatic scheduling,

- **Straighten progress line to period** will be covered in the Updating modules,

- Help files explains how these function operate:

  - **Tasks with no links**

  - **Tasks with only outgoing links**

  - **Compatibility**

  - **Options**

  - **Compute**

- The options set in the picture will result in the schedule calculating in a similar way to P6 and Microsoft Project.

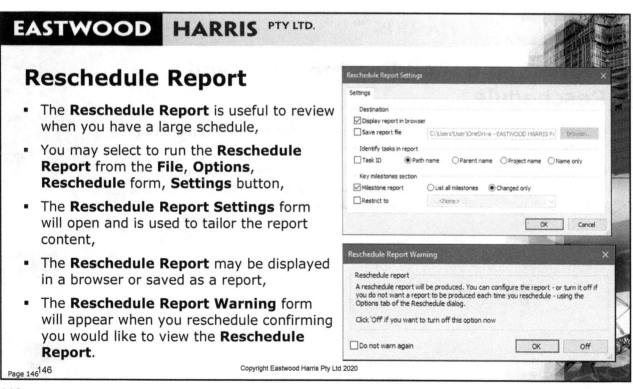

Page 145 145   Copyright Eastwood Harris Pty Ltd 2020

145

Reschedule Report

- The **Reschedule Report** is useful to review when you have a large schedule,

- You may select to run the **Reschedule Report** from the **File, Options, Reschedule** form, **Settings** button,

- The **Reschedule Report Settings** form will open and is used to tailor the report content,

- The **Reschedule Report** may be displayed in a browser or saved as a report,

- The **Reschedule Report Warning** form will appear when you reschedule confirming you would like to view the **Reschedule Report**.

Page 146 146   Copyright Eastwood Harris Pty Ltd 2020

146

6 - LINKING TASKS TO CREATE A CRITICAL PATH SCHEDULE - SUMMARY

- This module covered how to link tasks to create a critical path program, and

- Rescheduling a project,

- There are many **Reschedule Options** and some will not produce a Critical Path program,

- This course will not cover these options in detail but feel free to explore then in your own time,

- If you use the setting I recommend then the schedule will calculate in a similar way to other products and will create a Critical Path schedule,

- Once we have covered adding constraints we will have covered all the topics required to create a schedule in Powerproject.

147

Workshop 6 – Adding the Links and Reschedule

- You have determined the logical sequence of tasks, so you may now enter the links,

- After you have entered the links you should Reschedule the program if you do not have **Auto reschedule** switched on and this will calculate the Start and Finish dates and Total and Free floats.

148

EASTWOOD HARRIS PTY LTD.

7 – CONSTRAINTS

In this module we look at :

- How to add and remove constraints,
- Snapping
- Start on a New Day
- Partial Critical Path
- Float display and
- Negative float applies to chain.

Copyright Eastwood Harris Pty Ltd 2020

EASTWOOD HARRIS PTY LTD.

Understanding Constraints

- To correctly model the impact of events outside the logical sequence, you should use constraints,
- A constraint would be imposed to specific dates such as:
    - The availability of a facility to allow work to commence, or
    - The predetermined time a project must be complete by,
- Constraints in a schedule should be cross-referenced to Milestone Dates found in supporting documentation such as contract documentation or scope documents using **Task Notes** Function.

Copyright Eastwood Harris Pty Ltd 2020

EASTWOOD HARRIS PTY LTD.

Setting and Removing Constraints

- Constraints may be set on either the Start or Finish of tasks,
- To set a constraint when **Auto rescheduling** is not set:
  - Move the task to the required date position,
  - Right click on the task and select **Constraint Flag**,
  - Select the type of constraint from the list,
- A flag will appear on the task,
- To remove an existing constraint,
  - Select the constraint,
  - Right click and select **Remove**.

Copyright Eastwood Harris Pty Ltd 2020

Page 151¹⁵¹

151

EASTWOOD HARRIS PTY LTD.

Other ways to set Constraints

- Constraint may be set in when **Reschedule Options** is set to **Auto reschedule** either in:
- The **Properties View**, or
- The **Bar and Task Properties** form, or
- By showing the appropriate columns:

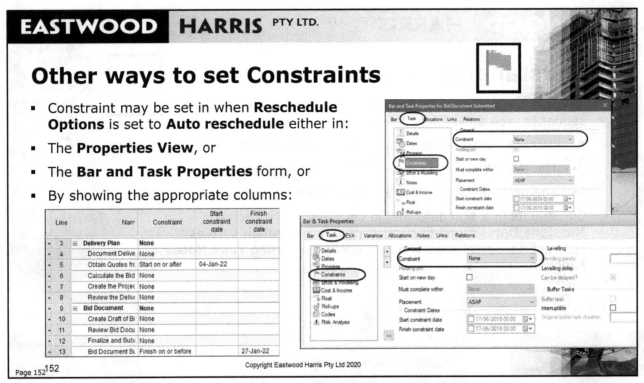

Copyright Eastwood Harris Pty Ltd 2020

Page 152¹⁵²

152

EASTWOOD **HARRIS** PTY LTD.

Types of Constraint

- A **Holding Pin** calculates like like an **Early Start** constraint:

    - It moves forward with the task but not backwards, when it is scheduled, or

    - Moves with the task when manually moved by dragging,

- A **Hard Constraint** means that the task is scheduled on that date and **Negative Float** is created on the predecessor when the predecessor finishes later than the **Hard Constraint** date,

- See picture on the next slide:

Picture	Link Name	Link Type
🚩	Start on or after	Soft
🚩	Start on	Hard
🏴	Finish on or before	Soft
🚩	Deadline	Soft
🏴	Finish on	Hard
🏳🏳	Work (schedule) between	Soft
📌	Holding pin	Moves with the task when manually moved

Copyright Eastwood Harris Pty Ltd 2020

EASTWOOD **HARRIS** PTY LTD.

Constraint Calculation

All products calculate differently,

- Powerproject **Start On** is a **Hard Constraint**,

- A P6 **Mandatory Start** is also **Hard** and calculates like a Powerproject **Start On**,

- A Microsoft Project **Must Start On** constraint is **Soft**, negative float is created but the tasks acknowledges the predecessor.

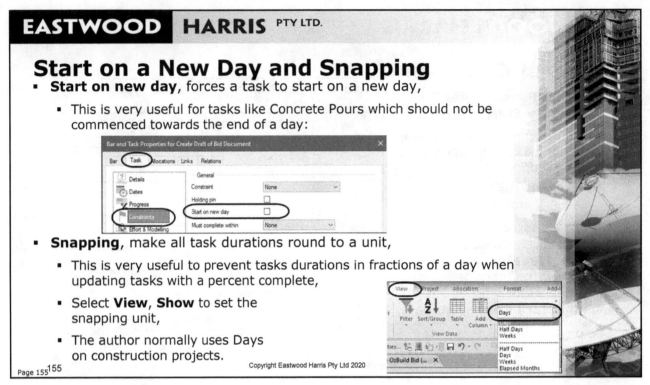

Start on a New Day and Snapping

- **Start on new day**, forces a task to start on a new day,

  - This is very useful for tasks like Concrete Pours which should not be commenced towards the end of a day:

- **Snapping**, make all task durations round to a unit,

  - This is very useful to prevent tasks durations in fractions of a day when updating tasks with a percent complete,

  - Select **View**, **Show** to set the snapping unit,

  - The author normally uses Days on construction projects.

Page 155 155   Copyright Eastwood Harris Pty Ltd 2020

155

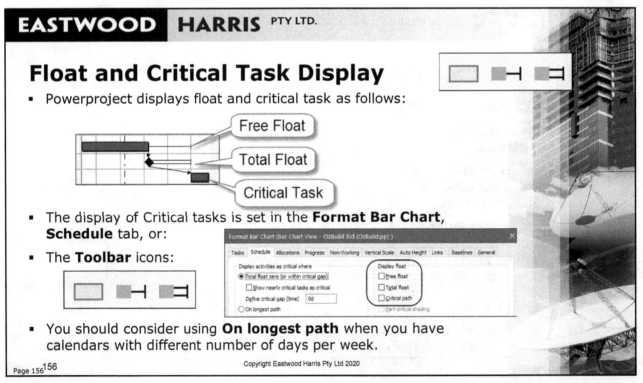

Float and Critical Task Display

- Powerproject displays float and critical task as follows:

  - Free Float
  - Total Float
  - Critical Task

- The display of Critical tasks is set in the **Format Bar Chart**, **Schedule** tab, or:

- The **Toolbar** icons:

- You should consider using **On longest path** when you have calendars with different number of days per week.

Page 156 156   Copyright Eastwood Harris Pty Ltd 2020

156

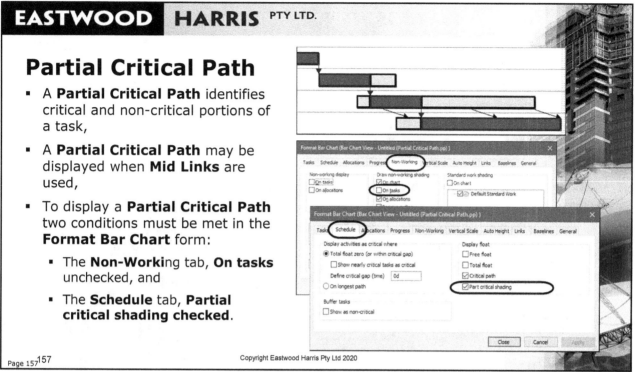

Partial Critical Path

- A **Partial Critical Path** identifies critical and non-critical portions of a task,

- A **Partial Critical Path** may be displayed when **Mid Links** are used,

- To display a **Partial Critical Path** two conditions must be met in the **Format Bar Chart** form:

  - The **Non-Working** tab, **On tasks** unchecked, and

  - The **Schedule** tab, **Partial critical shading checked**.

Copyright Eastwood Harris Pty Ltd 2020

157

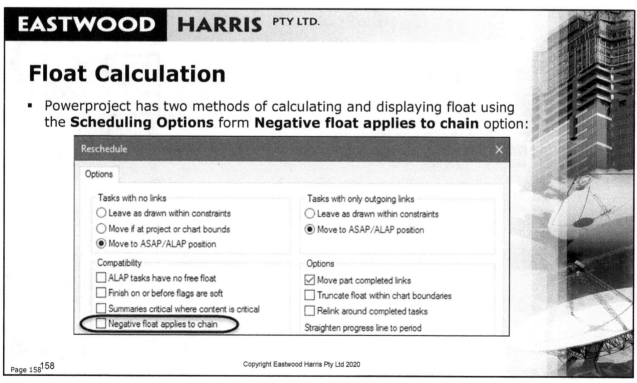

Float Calculation

- Powerproject has two methods of calculating and displaying float using the **Scheduling Options** form **Negative float applies to chain** option:

Copyright Eastwood Harris Pty Ltd 2020

158

EASTWOOD HARRIS PTY LTD.

Float Calculation

- **Negative float applies to chain option** unchecked:
  - Only the first task in a chain causing negative float is displayed with Negative Float and it also displays a Negative Float bar:

- **Negative float applies to chain option** checked:
  - All tasks in the chain calculate Negative Float but **NO** Negative Float bar is displayed against any task,
  - This is how P6 and Microsoft Project calculate, but they will both display a Negative Float bar,
  - Powerproject does NOT display a **Negative Float** bar with this option.

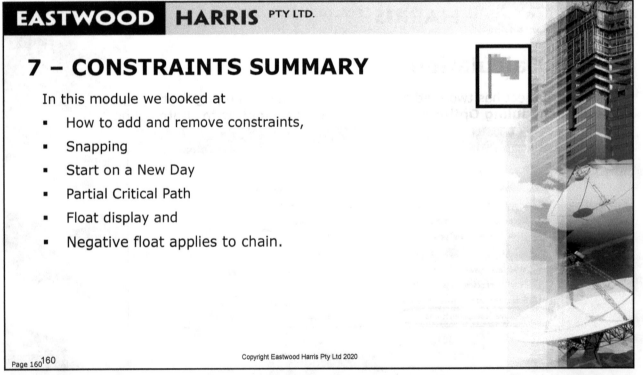

159

EASTWOOD HARRIS PTY LTD.

7 – CONSTRAINTS SUMMARY

In this module we looked at

- How to add and remove constraints,
- Snapping
- Start on a New Day
- Partial Critical Path
- Float display and
- Negative float applies to chain.

160

Workshop 7 - Constraints

- Management has provided further input to your schedule,
- You will need to set some constraints and eliminate Negative Float.

8 - OTHER TASK TYPES

This module will cover the following topics:

- Task-per-line mode
- Expanded Tasks
- Hammock Tasks
- Subheadings and
- Buffer Tasks.

EASTWOOD **HARRIS** PTY LTD.

Task-per-line mode

- Powerproject may display multiple tasks on line in the Gantt Chart,
- Powerproject terms this **Multiple Tasks on a Bar**,
- This is useful when it is desirable to reduce the number of lines in a program and when it would be logical to display them all on the same line,
- Powerproject may also display these tasks on separate lines if required,
- The picture below is an example of a housing project with each line representing a house with each trade represented by the tasks:

Copyright Eastwood Harris Pty Ltd 2020

Page 163 163

163

EASTWOOD **HARRIS** PTY LTD.

Understanding Bars and Tasks

- When you create multiple tasks on one line the two terms you need to understand are **Bar** and **Task**,

- A **Bar** contains one or more **Tasks**:

  - **The Bar Name** is displayed in the **Name** column when the Tasks are rolled up,

- **Tasks** may be drawn on the Gantt Chart:

  - There may be multiple **Tasks** to a **Bar**,

  - The **Task Name** is displayed in the Name multiple Tasks is expanded.

Copyright Eastwood Harris Pty Ltd 2020

Page 164 164

164

EASTWOOD | **HARRIS** PTY LTD.

Adding Task-per-line

- You may create multiple tasks on one line by dragging in the Gantt Chart and then enter the **Bar** name in the **Name** column:

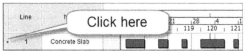

- Click the + button to the left of the line number within the table and enter each **Task** name in the **Name** column,

Line	Name	January					Fe
		7	14	21	28	4	11
		116	117	118	119	120	121
1	Form						
2	Reo						
3	Pour						
4	Cure						
5	Strip						

- Click the - button to return the tasks to one line mode.

165

EASTWOOD | **HARRIS** PTY LTD.

Understand the Difference Between Bars and Task

- When there are multiple Tasks-per-line:
  - The **Bar** description is seen in the **Name** column when the tasks **ARE** on one line,
  - The **Task** description is seen in the **Name** column when the tasks **ARE** NOT on one line,
  - The **Bar** description is Concrete Slab,

  - The **Tasks** are Form, Reo, Pour etc.:

166

81

EASTWOOD HARRIS PTY LTD.

Task-per-line "Inherited Links"

- By default Tasks on one line have an inherited Finish-to-Start link between tasks and no link is required, and the tasks will run consecutively,

- **Note:** This mode may not be considered a **Critical Path** schedule as tasks are not linked,

- It is possible to draw links between tasks on the same bar but this will ensure a delay or interval between them,

- **Note**: **Negative Lags** will not calculate unless the **Bar** option **Tasks may Overlap** is checked, see next slide.

EASTWOOD HARRIS PTY LTD.

Tasks may overlap

- The **Tasks may overlap** option is found on the **Bar & Task Properties**, **Details** tab or on the Gantt Chart right click menu,

- There are no inherited links for multiple tasks assigned to a bar when this option is checked:

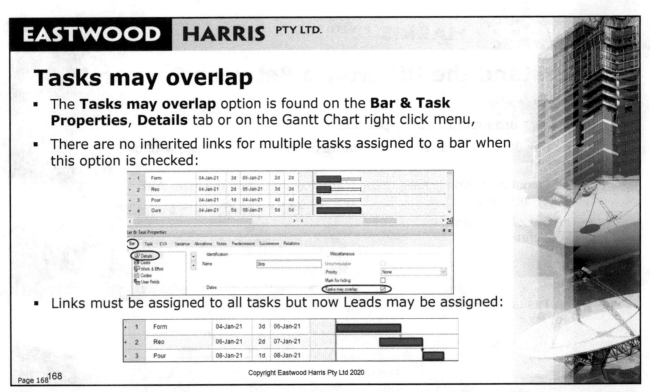

- Links must be assigned to all tasks but now Leads may be assigned:

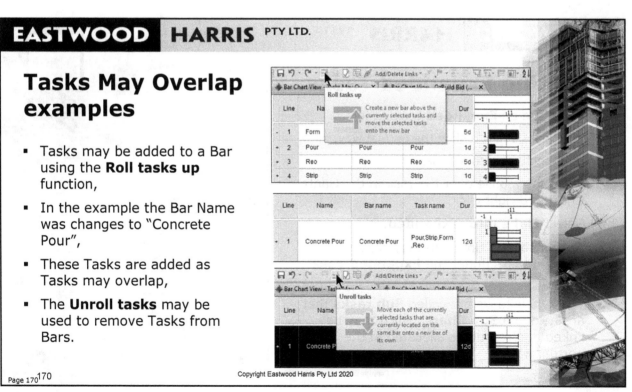

EASTWOOD HARRIS PTY LTD.

Expanded Tasks

- **Expanded** tasks allow detailed planning to be hidden in turn allowing the uncluttering of a view with the detail readily available,

- They **DO NOT** operate like Microsoft Project Summary Tasks or P6 Hammocks,

- Expanded tasks are displayed as a normal task but the detailed tasks may be hidden and are held in a **Sub Chart**,

- The **Project View** displays **Expanded Tasks** nodes:

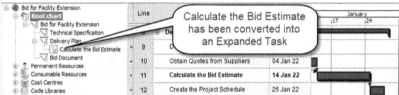

- Existing tasks may be converted into **Expanded** tasks and detail added below them or on new ones created,

- Tasks under an **Expanded Task** are called **Subtasks**.

171

EASTWOOD HARRIS PTY LTD.

Creating Expanded Tasks...

- To create an **Expanded** task either:
  - Create a new task in the normal way, or
  - Select an existing task,

- Place the mouse over the task in the Gantt Chart and right click,

- Select **Make into**, **Expanded**,

- At this point in time you may create detailed tasks under the **Expanded Task** and

- These new tasks are called **Sub tasks** that are held in a **Sub Chart**, which may be linked and resources allocated in the normal way.

Cut	Ctrl+X	
Copy	Ctrl+C	
Delete	Del	
Enter Progress...		
Progress Up To	▶	
Progress from Allocations		
Calculate Task Weightings		
Unlink Tasks	Ctrl+Shift+F2	
Constraint Flag	▶	
Split/Join		
Make Into	▶	Task
Linking	▶	Start Milestone
Mark for Hiding		Finish Milestone
Copy Allocations to Group...		Summary
Assignment View		Expanded
Assign	▶	Hammock
Open as Chart		Buffer Task
Add to Hammock...		Interruptible
Remove from Hammock		
Copy to Task Pool		
Is a Project		
Book Out...		
Copy Properties to Defaults		
Properties...	Alt+Enter	

172

Creating Sub Tasks under an Expanded Task

- The "Calculate the Bid Estimate" task becomes a new chart in the project hierarchy,

- To access the new chart either:

  - Left click to select the **Sub Chart** from the **Project View**, or

  - Double click on the task bar in the Bar Chart,

- Now you may create and link the new tasks, which are called **Sub tasks**, in the new Expanded task **Sub Chart**,

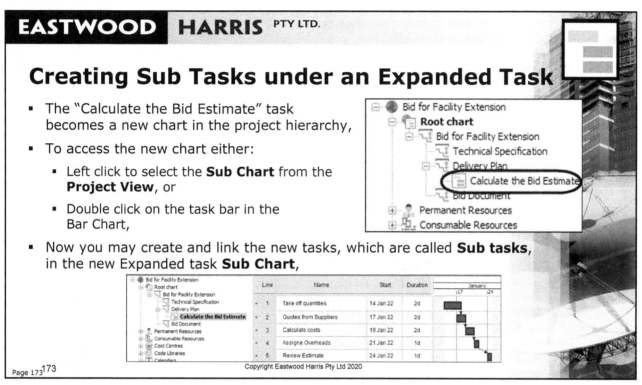

Copyright Eastwood Harris Pty Ltd 2020

173

Displaying the Expanded and Project tasks but not the Sub Tasks:

- Click on **Root chart** in the **Project View** and all tasks except the **Expanded task Sub tasks** are displayed,

- Other nodes in **Project View**, except the **Expanded** task node, may be selected and the **Expanded** task **Sub tasks** will not be displayed:

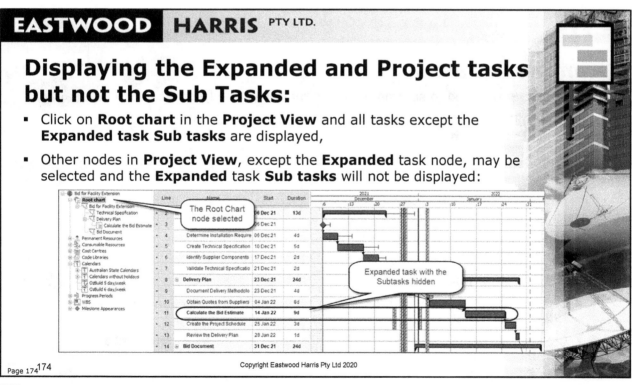

Copyright Eastwood Harris Pty Ltd 2020

174

EASTWOOD HARRIS PTY LTD.

Displaying Expanded tasks Sub tasks and Project tasks together:

- Select the required nodes in the **Project View** in order to display the **Expanded** tasks **Sub tasks** with other project tasks on one screen,

- Now all tasks associated with the selected nodes are displayed and links may be made between any tasks:

Page 175¹⁷⁵ Copyright Eastwood Harris Pty Ltd 2020

175

EASTWOOD HARRIS PTY LTD.

Hammock

Hammock Tasks

- **Hammocks** are used to summarise tasks that are not adjacent to each other,

- Unlike P6, Powerproject **Hammock** tasks do not have **Links** to the tasks assigned to the **Hammock**,

- **Hammock** start and finish dates are taken from the earliest and latest dates of their assigned tasks,

- **Hammock** durations are back calculated from the task dates over the calendar assigned to the Hammock,

- Expanding a **Hammock** will display the assigned tasks twice, in the chart and under the hammock,

- To create a **Hammock**, either:

    - Select an empty bar of your project by clicking on the line number, then select **Home**, **Insert – Hammock**, and enter the Hammock name, or

    - Draw a task, name it and then Right Click on the bar and select **Make into**, **Hammock**.

Page 176¹⁷⁶ Copyright Eastwood Harris Pty Ltd 2020

176

EASTWOOD HARRIS PTY LTD.

Assigning tasks to a Hammock:

- Select the tasks to be added to a **Hammock**,

- Right click and select **Add to Hammock...**,

- Select the required **Hammock** and click **OK**,

- Tasks may be assigned to multiple **Hammocks**,

- **Hammock** tasks are displayed in two places:

  - In its original position, and

  - A copy of the task is displayed under the hammock when it is expanded by clicking on the + by the Name:

- To remove tasks from a **Hammock**, Right click and select **Remove from Hammock**.

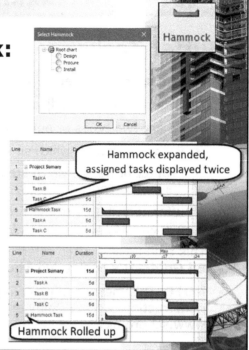

Hammock expanded, assigned tasks displayed twice

Hammock Rolled up

177

EASTWOOD HARRIS PTY LTD.

Subheadings

- A **Subheading** is a **Bar Name** without tasks,

- A task name may be entered and no task bar drawn on the Gantt Chart or duration entered,

Line	Name	Start	Duration	Finish	May				June	
					13	20	27	3	10	17
					135	136	137	138	139	
1	First Task Name	20/05/19	3d	22/05/19	1					
2	Second Task	24/05/19	1w 2d	03/06/19		2				
	SUB HEADING									
3	Third Task	03/06/19	1w 3d	12/06/19				3		
4	Fourth Task	14/06/19	3d	18/06/19					4	

- This text then becomes a **Subheading**,

- This is useful if you have a long list of tasks under a Summary task and you do not want to add any more lower level Summary tasks, but you want to group them under headings,

- **Note**: A **Subheading** may also be created by a band heading create by grouping tasks by a code.

178

EASTWOOD HARRIS PTY LTD.

Buffer Tasks

- **Buffer tasks** are used to show and manage the contingent time,
- Their duration is self adjusting,
- There are two types of buffer tasks:
    - **Feeder buffers** – which sit within the project protecting key dates, and
    - **Project buffers** – which are usually the last task in a project protecting the project end date,
- A buffer contributes to the Critical Path calculation, but when its start date is affected it will shrink (or expand) and protect the Critical Path,
- This technique is often referred to as **Critical Chain Scheduling**, see **Eli Goldratt's** book titled **Theory of Constraints**.
- **NOTE:** This method of planning is supported by the Society of Construction Laws' – Delay and Disruption Protocol – October 2002 (see www.scl.org.uk).

Page 179 179   Copyright Eastwood Harris Pty Ltd 2020

179

EASTWOOD HARRIS PTY LTD.

How to create a Buffer Task

- To create a **Buffer task**,
    - Create a task in the normal way,
    - Link the task into the project and reschedule the project so the tasks have the correct dates,
    - Right Click on the task and select to **Make into**, **Buffer Task**.

Page 180 180   Copyright Eastwood Harris Pty Ltd 2020

180

EASTWOOD HARRIS PTY LTD.

8 - OTHER TASK TYPES SUMMARY

In this module will covered the following topics:

- Task-per-line mode
- Expanded Tasks
- Hammock Tasks
- Subheadings and
- Buffer Tasks.

Copyright Eastwood Harris Pty Ltd 2020

181

EASTWOOD HARRIS PTY LTD.

Workshop 8 – Other Task Types

- This workshop will take you through the process of creating the following in your schedule:
    - Task-per-line mode
    - Expanded Tasks
    - Hammock Tasks
    - Subheadings where Bar Names are used as Headers Only
- Before you move on to the next workshop delete all of the tasks you create in this workshop.

Copyright Eastwood Harris Pty Ltd 2020

182

EASTWOOD HARRIS PTY LTD.

9 - FORMATTING THE DISPLAY

We will cover in this module formatting:

- The Date Zone, Gridlines, Vertical Shading and Multiple Date Zones,
- Hiding non-working time,
- Formatting bars and Links,
- Adding Notes,
- Link Categories,
- Columns, Date and Durations,
- Tables and Views,
- Adding Annotations
- Task Numbering.

Page 183

183

EASTWOOD HARRIS PTY LTD.

Introduction to Views

- Project data is displayed using a **View** and any formatting changes are editing a **View**, or an attribute associated to **View**, such as a **Table**, **Filter** or **Sort/Group**,

- A **View** holds the following formatting:

  - **Date Zone**
  - **Gantt Chart**

- Other attributes associated with a **View**, such as **Tables**, **Filters** or **Sort/Groups** may be assigned to multiple views, and edited without the associated view being displayed,

- **NOTE:** The **Undo** button does not undo formatting changes, only calculations and data changes.

184

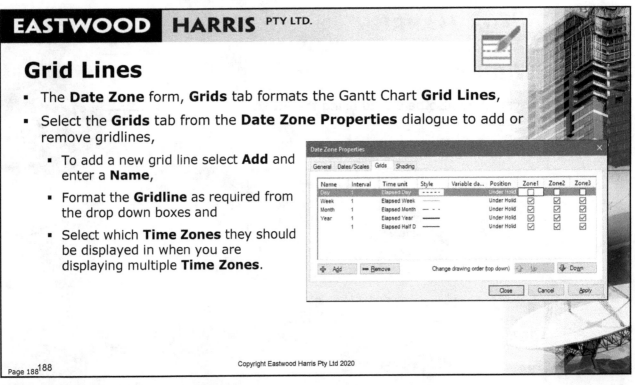

EASTWOOD HARRIS PTY LTD.

Editing Date Zone Rulers

- Up to 10 **Date Zone Rulers** may be displayed,
- The picture is displaying 6,
- To format the **Date Zone** Rulers:
  - Open the **Date Zone Properties** form,
  - Add or remove **Rulers** from the right hand side of the **General** tab by selecting a **Type**,
  - Then select **Time Unit** and **Quantity**, and
  - Reformat from the bottom of the form as required.

EASTWOOD HARRIS PTY LTD.

Grid Lines

- The **Date Zone** form, **Grids** tab formats the Gantt Chart **Grid Lines**,
- Select the **Grids** tab from the **Date Zone Properties** dialogue to add or remove gridlines,
  - To add a new grid line select **Add** and enter a **Name**,
  - Format the **Gridline** as required from the drop down boxes and
  - Select which **Time Zones** they should be displayed in when you are displaying multiple **Time Zones**.

EASTWOOD HARRIS PTY LTD.

Day, Week and Month Numbering

- Powerproject allows **Day**, **Week** or **Month** numbering using the **Elapsed units** option in the **Date Zone Properties** form, **General** tab:

- The **Date Zero** is where numbering is commenced and will default to the **Project start date** when the project is created,

- To align **Date Zero** to another date:
  - Open the **Date Zone Properties** form,
  - Select the **Dates/Scales** tab,
  - Select the **Date Zero** from the drop box,
  - Select **Close**.

Copyright Eastwood Harris Pty Ltd 2020

189

EASTWOOD HARRIS PTY LTD.

Vertical Shading

- The **Date Zone** form, **Shading** tab formats the Gantt Chart,

- Like P6, vertical shading may be placed behind the tasks to represent Shut Down time etc., to add shading:
  - Select the **Date Zone Properties** form **Shading** tab,
  - Select **Add** to add a Shading,
  - Enter the **Shading Start** and **Finish** dates or a **Variable Date** from the list and format the colour:

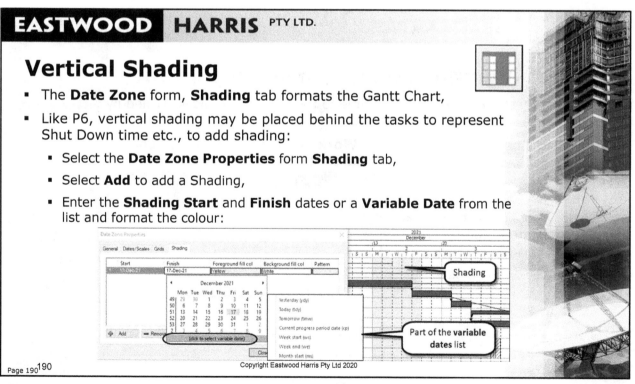

Copyright Eastwood Harris Pty Ltd 2020

190

93

EASTWOOD HARRIS PTY LTD.

Multiple Date Zones

- The **Date Zone** may be divided into two or three different zones each with a different scales,

					2004		
	January					February	
5	12	19	26 2 9	16			23
1	2	3	4 5 6	7			

- This is similar to the **SureTrak Zoomed Timescale** function,
  - Place the mouse in the **Date Zone** where you want the second or third new **Date Zone** to start,
  - Right click and select **Start New Scale Zone**,
- A grey line will indicate the start of the new **Date Zone**,
- Now each time scale may be formatted individually,
- To remove **Zone 2** or **Zone 3**, right click in the **Date Zone** and select to **Remove This Scale Zone**.

191

EASTWOOD HARRIS PTY LTD.

Displaying and Hiding non-working time

- Powerproject allows non working time to be hidden and this is termed by Powerproject as **Folded Out of View**,
- It is often best to ensure that **Non Working** time is not displayed but you need to ensure your **Folding Calendar** does not fold work time out of view,
- Thus if you have 5d/w and a 6d/w calendars, then make the **Folding Calendar** the 6d/w calendar,
- Examples on the next slide.

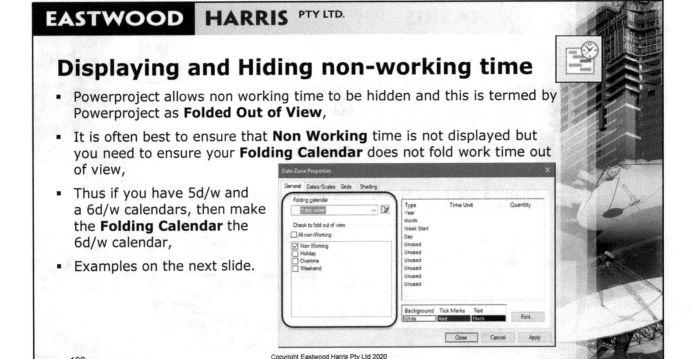

192

EASTWOOD HARRIS PTY LTD.

Hiding non-working time examples

- No working time hidden and timescale shows full 24 hours: **Note: Driving Links** are not vertical,

- Non Working time hidden, so only 08:00 to 16:00 is displayed and **Driving Links** become vertical:

- Weekends hidden on a 5 day/week **Folding calendar**:

- Holidays hidden:

Sat and Sun hidden   Holidays

Holidays hidden

Copyright Eastwood Harris Pty Ltd 2020

EASTWOOD HARRIS PTY LTD.

Formatting the Bar Chart

- Powerproject formatting is in most areas more functional than P6 and MSP and in a few areas less,

- For example Powerproject links may be coloured and non work time displayed according to each tasks' calendar, but Float bars and the Critical Path may not be formatted, just displayed or hidden,

- Most formatting options are on the **Format** tab,

- When the icon has a highlighted background the attribute is being displayed:

- Keyboard short cuts may used to format the Gantt Chart.

Copyright Eastwood Harris Pty Ltd 2020

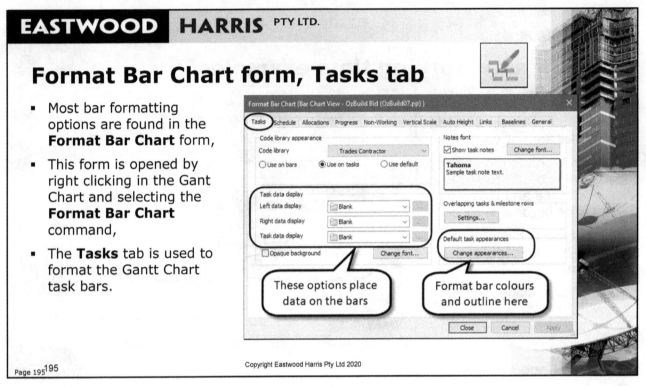

Format Bar Chart form, Tasks tab

- Most bar formatting options are found in the **Format Bar Chart** form,

- This form is opened by right clicking in the Gant Chart and selecting the **Format Bar Chart** command,

- The **Tasks** tab is used to format the Gantt Chart task bars.

Page 195 195

195

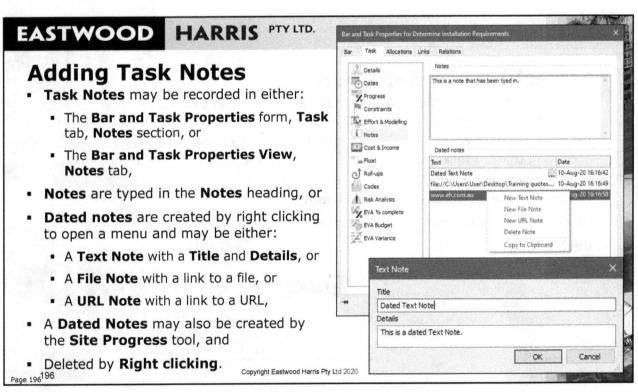

Adding Task Notes

- **Task Notes** may be recorded in either:
  - The **Bar and Task Properties** form, **Task** tab, **Notes** section, or
  - The **Bar and Task Properties View**, **Notes** tab,

- **Notes** are typed in the **Notes** heading, or

- **Dated notes** are created by right clicking to open a menu and may be either:
  - A **Text Note** with a **Title** and **Details**, or
  - A **File Note** with a link to a file, or
  - A **URL Note** with a link to a URL,

- A **Dated Notes** may also be created by the **Site Progress** tool, and

- Deleted by **Right clicking**.

Page 196 196

196

EASTWOOD HARRIS PTY LTD.

Displaying Task Notes

- When the **Format Bar Chart** form, **Task** tab, **Show task notes** check box is checked then a yellow indicator is displayed in the top right corner of a task bar indicating a task has been assigned either a **Note** or a **Dated Text Note** and

- When there are multiple **Task Notes** then only the first **Task Note** is displayed in a pop up window when the cursor is placed on the task,

- **URL Notes** and **File Notes** do not display a yellow indicator.

Task Note Indicator

This is a Note

Page 197 197   Copyright Eastwood Harris Pty Ltd 2020

197

EASTWOOD HARRIS PTY LTD.

Format Bar Chart, Schedule tab

- Free float, Total float and Critical path boxes display these bars:

- **Note:** The Free float, Total float bars and the Critical path display may not be formatted,

- **Longest Path** should be used with multiple calendars,

- **Partial critical shading** was covered with **Mid Links**.

Page 198 198   Copyright Eastwood Harris Pty Ltd 2020

198

EASTWOOD HARRIS PTY LTD.

Link Categories

- **Link Categories** are created and formatted in the **Library Explorer**, and in turn assigned to Links,

- Links may be hidden from view by **Link Category** using the **Format Bar Chart** form, **Links** tab:

- Selected **Link Categories** may be ignored in schedule calculations from the **Reschedule**, **Options** form,

- **Note: Ignoring Link Categories** allows different build options in one schedule, such as East to West or West to East, or one or two crane options. This may save the requirement for two schedules when the task are the same for two options.

Page 199 199

Copyright Eastwood Harris Pty Ltd 2020

199

EASTWOOD HARRIS PTY LTD.

Formatting the Spreadsheet using the Table function

- The formatting of the spreadsheet is achieved through the **Table** function,

- The **Table** formatting functions have far more options than P6 or Microsoft Project:

  - Each date column may be formatted with a different date format,

  - Most Baseline data fields may be viewed in columns,

  - Columns may be created to display the data for one resource only and the resource data may be updated in a column,

- **Note:** The default **Column title** does not indicate that it is displaying baseline data, so when a baseline column is displayed the user must change the **Column title** so it is clear that it is displaying baseline data.

Page 200 200

Copyright Eastwood Harris Pty Ltd 2020

200

EASTWOOD HARRIS PTY LTD.

Adding Columns...

- To add a column right click on an existing column heading and select **Add Column**,

- You are now editing a **Table** that may also be assigned to another **View**,

- Select a field from the menu (the categories are very different from P6 and MSP),

- A column is now added into the spreadsheet:

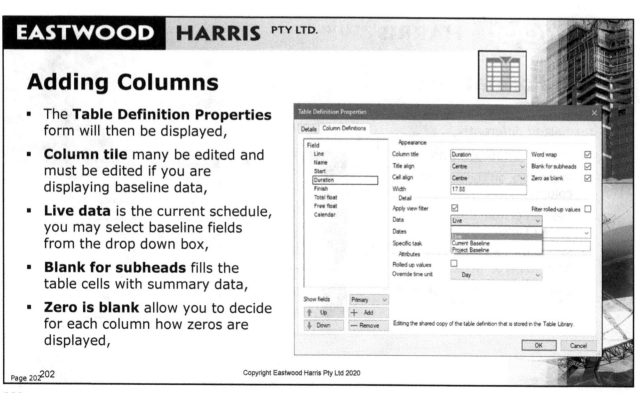

Copyright Eastwood Harris Pty Ltd 2020

201

EASTWOOD HARRIS PTY LTD.

Adding Columns

- The **Table Definition Properties** form will then be displayed,

- **Column tile** many be edited and must be edited if you are displaying baseline data,

- **Live data** is the current schedule, you may select baseline fields from the drop down box,

- **Blank for subheads** fills the table cells with summary data,

- **Zero is blank** allow you to decide for each column how zeros are displayed,

Copyright Eastwood Harris Pty Ltd 2020

202

Date Format...

- The date format displayed dialogue boxes is normally adopted from your **System Date format** set in **System Short Date** from **Start**, **Settings**, **Time** and **Language**,

- The date format is also further formatted using the **File**, **Options**, **Format** tab,

- This is where you may opt to display the time with the date,

- The setting displayed are the authors preference.

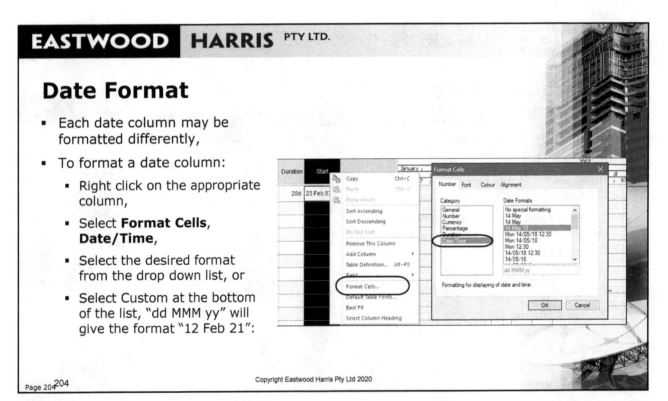

Page 203 203

Copyright Eastwood Harris Pty Ltd 2020

203

Date Format

- Each date column may be formatted differently,

- To format a date column:

  - Right click on the appropriate column,

  - Select **Format Cells**, **Date/Time**,

  - Select the desired format from the drop down list, or

  - Select Custom at the bottom of the list, "dd MMM yy" will give the format "12 Feb 21":

Page 204 204

Copyright Eastwood Harris Pty Ltd 2020

204

EASTWOOD HARRIS PTY LTD.

Duration Format...

- The duration format is complex and the best thing to do is play with the settings until you understand it or get what you want,

- It is initially formatted for a project in the **File**, **Options**, **Format** tab,

- The setting displayed is the authors preferred:

Options for OzBuild Workshop

Edit   Assign   View   Format   Progress   Reschedule   File Locations   Calendars   Spreadsheet   General

Show time with dates
☐ Annotations   ☑ Dialogs   ☐ Spreadsheet

Date format
◉ Short format   ○ Long format

Duration format
○ Decimal (4.4w)   ◉ Mixed time units (4w 2d)   ○ Compact (4:2)
Maximum number of mixed time units displayed in a duration   [2]

Work Breakdown Structure format
Path separator   [.]

Formulae
Date constant format   [Regional default ▾]

Properties
Decimal places for User Fields   [2]

[Close]

Page 205 205   Copyright Eastwood Harris Pty Ltd 2020

205

EASTWOOD HARRIS PTY LTD.

Duration Format...

- The duration format of days, weeks etc, is set in the **Format Cells** form and may be set differently for each column,

- When an **Override time** unit is set in the **Table Definition Properties** form then this format takes preference over the **Format Cells** setting:

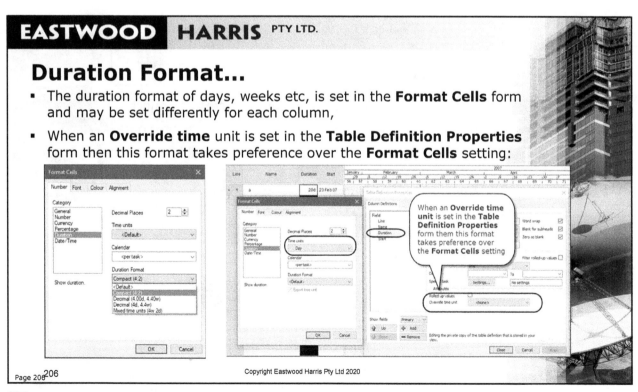

When an **Override time** unit is set in the **Table Definition Properties** form them this format takes preference over the **Format Cells** setting

Page 206 206   Copyright Eastwood Harris Pty Ltd 2020

206

Duration Format

- The Duration of Milestones may be displayed either:
  - As a number, e.g. 0 d, or
  - As a blank:

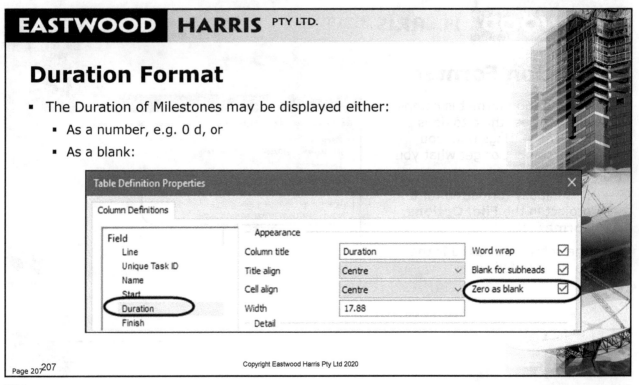

Page 207207

207

Saving the Table

- Tables of columns may be saved in the same way as Microsoft Project,
- Tables are created to display different data and reapplied at a later date,
- You may create a new table and edit it, or edit an existing table and then save as a new table,
- To create a new **Table**,
  - Select the **View** group, **Table**, **Save as**,
  - Give your **Table** a new name,
  - To switch between different tables select **View**, **Table** and select the table you require from the list of saved tables:

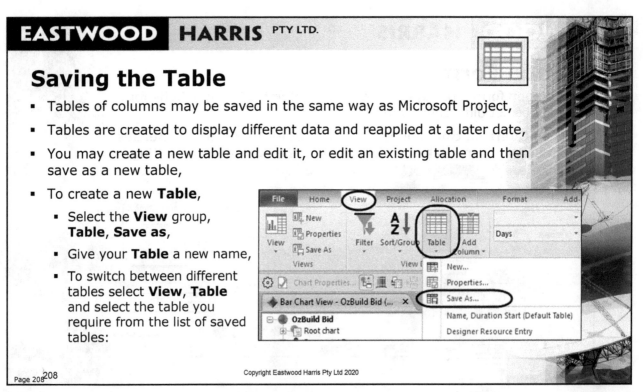

Page 208208

208

EASTWOOD HARRIS PTY LTD.

Creating and Saving Views

- Views in Powerproject work in a similar way to Microsoft Project,
- A **View** holds the **Gantt Chart** and **Timescale** formatting and is assigned a **Group and Sort** and a **Table**, and may have a **Filter** assigned,
- After changing a View, say by assigning a different table, it may be saved by saving the project or a new View create using **Save View**,
- Each View may display project data with different formatting,
- To save the view:
  - On the **View** tab, **Views** group, **Save As**,
  - Give your **View** a name,
  - A **View Category** will show the new View sub menu,
- Applying another View will open the View in another window.

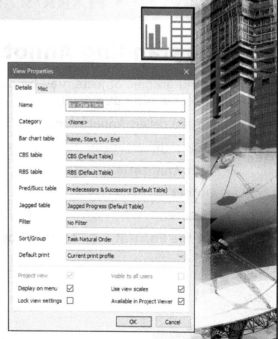

Copyright Eastwood Harris Pty Ltd 2020

209

EASTWOOD HARRIS PTY LTD.

Editing a View...

- The **View Properties** form may be used to edit views,

- A **View** includes the bar and timescale formatting and these are not edited here,
- The assigned **Bar Chart Table**, **Filter** and **Sort/Group**, plus other attributes, may be changed here,
- A **View** assigned a **View Category** will be then be displayed in a **View** submenu.

Copyright Eastwood Harris Pty Ltd 2020

210

Editing a View

- **Display on menu** means the View is displayed on the first menu drop down list, if it is not checked then you have to select **More Views...** to access the View,

- **Lock view setting** means that if you change a view and save the project the View changes are not saved, this stops you messing up important views,

- **Use view scales** means that the same timescale is applied to **Subcharts**,

- Available to **Project Viewer** means that a person opening the file in **Project Viewer** will have access to this view, thus enabling you to restrict what people may see in **Project Viewer**.

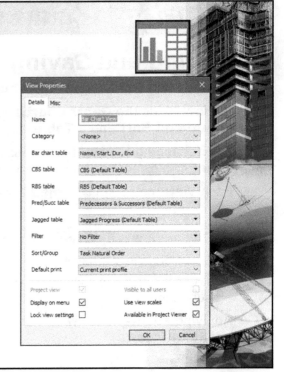

Copyright Eastwood Harris Pty Ltd 2020

211

Understanding Annotations

- Text and graphic objects may be placed on the Gantt Chart for reporting and presentation purposes,

- These are called Annotations,

- There are three types:

  - **Text Annotation**

  - **Object**

  - **Picture**

- Select the **Format** tab, **Annotations** to insert an **Annotation**.

Copyright Eastwood Harris Pty Ltd 2020

212

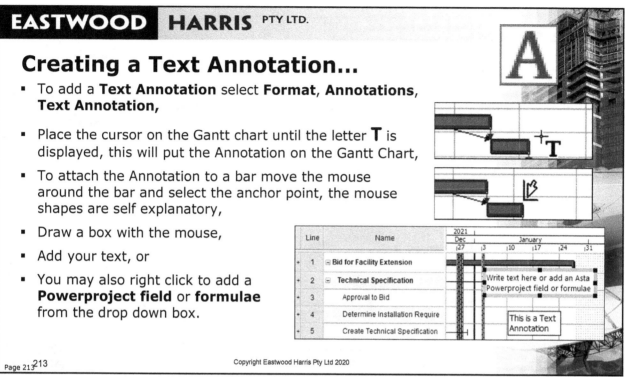

Creating a Text Annotation...

- To add a **Text Annotation** select **Format**, **Annotations**, **Text Annotation**,

- Place the cursor on the Gantt chart until the letter **T** is displayed, this will put the Annotation on the Gantt Chart,

- To attach the Annotation to a bar move the mouse around the bar and select the anchor point, the mouse shapes are self explanatory,

- Draw a box with the mouse,

- Add your text, or

- You may also right click to add a **Powerproject field** or **formulae** from the drop down box.

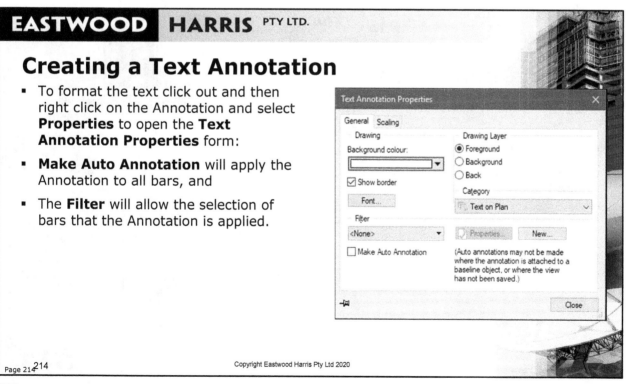

Creating a Text Annotation

- To format the text click out and then right click on the Annotation and select **Properties** to open the **Text Annotation Properties** form:

- **Make Auto Annotation** will apply the Annotation to all bars, and

- The **Filter** will allow the selection of bars that the Annotation is applied.

EASTWOOD HARRIS PTY LTD.

Creating an Object Annotation

- Click the **Object** annotation toolbar button or go to **Insert**, **Object**,

  - Place the cursor on the Gantt Chart,
  - Draw a box,
  - The **Insert Object** form will open allowing linking to an Object:

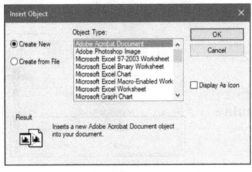

Copyright Eastwood Harris Pty Ltd 2020

215

EASTWOOD HARRIS PTY LTD.

Picture Annotation

- Select **Format**, **Annotations**, **Picture** to add a graphic to the Gantt Chart,
- Browse and add a graphic,
- To re-size the picture click on it and use the resizing arrows, or use the hand to reposition a picture:

Copyright Eastwood Harris Pty Ltd 2020

216

Project Task ID or (WBN) Number Definition

- You may number your task with a hierarchal numbering system called **Task ID (WBN)** numbering,

- The **Project**, **Properties**, **Project Task ID or (WBN) Number Definition** form is used to define or renumber the structure,

- It is probably better to use the newer WBS function if you wish to show a Hierarchical WBS structure:

Task ID (WBN) Numbering

Project Task ID (WBN) Numbering Definition

Definition
☐ Disable Task IDs (WBN)

Range	Start value	Increment	Minimum width
0 ---- 9	0100	100	4

Pathname separator ☐   Task separator ☐   Task ID (WBN) Prefix ☐

Uniqueness
Task IDs (WBN) are
○ Unique
◉ Unique within Summary / Expanded Task
○ Not unique
☐ Allow tasks on same bar to share codes

Renumber
☐ Perform renumbering on selection
☐ Renumber inside selected summary / expanded tasks
☐ Skip over Task ID (WBN) clashes

OK   Cancel

217

Unique Task ID Numbering

- A **Unique Task ID** may be assigned in a similar method to Oracle Primavera P6 Activity ID using the **Unique Task ID Numbering** function,

- This is best set up before you add tasks,

- Then they may be renumbered using the **Unique Task ID Numbering** function:

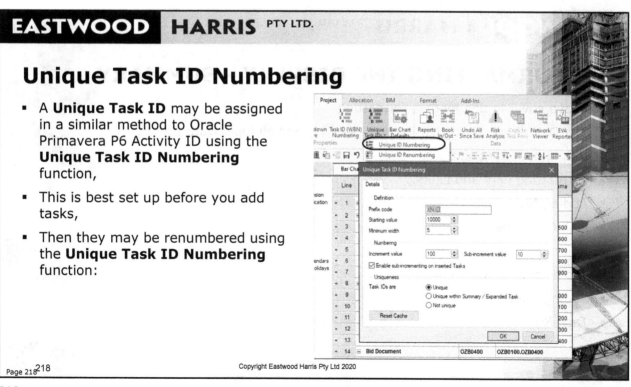

218

107

EASTWOOD HARRIS PTY LTD.

Displaying Task ID or (WBN) or Unique Task IDs

- Display the following columns to display the Task ID (WBN) codes:
  - **Unique task ID**
  - **Task ID (WBN), and**
  - **Task ID (WBN) Pathname:**

Line	Name	Unique task ID	Task ID (WBN)	Task ID (WBN) path name
1	⊟ Technical Specification	OZ1000	17100	17000.17100
2	Approval to Bid	OZ1010	15500	17000.17100.15500
3	Determine Installation Requirements	OZ1020	15600	17000.17100.15600
4	Create Technical Specification	OZ1030	15700	17000.17100.15700
5	Identify Supplier Components	OZ1040	15800	17000.17100.15800
6	Validate Technical Specification	OZ1050	15900	17000.17100.15900
7	⊟ Delivery Plan	OZ1060	17200	17000.17200
8	Document Delivery Methodology	OZ1070	16000	17000.17200.16000

EASTWOOD HARRIS PTY LTD.

9 - FORMATTING THE DISPLAY - SUMMARY

We have cover in this module formatting:

- The Date Zone, Gridlines, Vertical Shading and Multiple Date Zones,
- Hiding non-working time,
- Formatting bars and Links,
- Adding Notes,
- Link Categories,
- Columns, Date and Durations,
- Tables and Views,
- Adding Annotations
- Task Numbering.

EASTWOOD HARRIS PTY LTD.

Workshop 9 - Formatting the Bar Chart

- We will make some changes to the View to practise some of the skills covered in this module.

221

EASTWOOD **HARRIS** PTY LTD.

10 - CODE LIBRARIES

In this module we will cover:

- Creating Code Libraries,
- Assigning Codes to Tasks,
- Selecting which Code is displayed on task bars,
- Introduction to filters.

222

EASTWOOD HARRIS PTY LTD.

Understanding Code Libraries

- Code Libraries in Powerproject are similar to Activity Codes in P6 and Outline Codes in MSP, but are more powerful than either of the P6 and MSP functions.

  - Tasks may be coloured by a Code (like P6 Visualizer) and

  - Tasks may be assigned multiple Codes, unlike P6 or MSP,

  - **Note:** Assigning multiple codes to a task is useful for situations such as when 3 building floor codes may be assigned to a column task that spans three floors,

- Codes are created in the **Library Explorer**,

- Codes may be assigned in a number of ways but typically by dragging from the **Project View**,

- Codes may also be assigned from columns or from the **Bar & Task Properties** view or form,

- Powerproject Version 15 allows multiple code colouring of tasks with restrictions.

Page 223 223

223

EASTWOOD HARRIS PTY LTD.

Creating a New Code Library

- This example demonstrates the creation of a Responsibility Code Library,

  - Click the **Library Explorer** toolbar button,

  - Click on the **Code Library** folder in the left window of **Library Explorer**:

  - Right click in a blank part of the screen and select **New Code Library**,

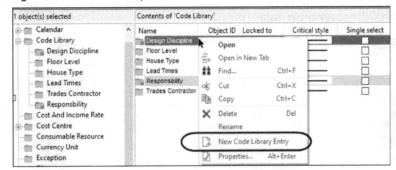

  - The picture above shows a new Code titled **Responsibility**.

Page 224 224

224

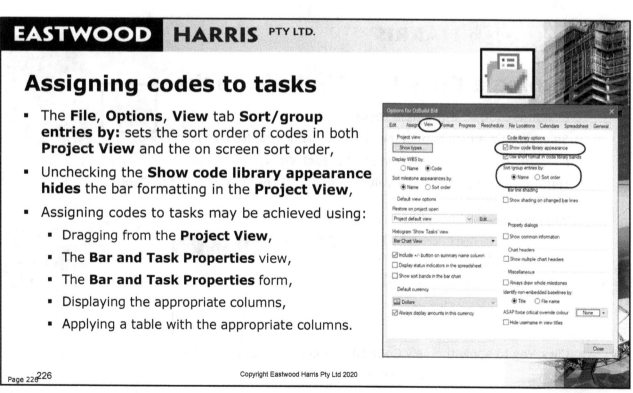

EASTWOOD HARRIS PTY LTD.

Creating New Codes

- Double click on the code folder to open it,

- Right click in the right hand pane and choose **New Code Library Entry**,

- Double click on the new entry and complete the form,

- The **Sort Order** column allows an alternative sort order for the Code display in both the **Project View** and on the screen,

- Unless you require your codes to always be sorted alphabetically you should use the **Sort order** option.

Page 225225

Copyright Eastwood Harris Pty Ltd 2020

225

EASTWOOD HARRIS PTY LTD.

Assigning codes to tasks

- The **File**, **Options**, **View** tab **Sort/group entries by:** sets the sort order of codes in both **Project View** and the on screen sort order,

- Unchecking the **Show code library appearance hides** the bar formatting in the **Project View**,

- Assigning codes to tasks may be achieved using:

    - Dragging from the **Project View**,

    - The **Bar and Task Properties** view,

    - The **Bar and Task Properties** form,

    - Displaying the appropriate columns,

    - Applying a table with the appropriate columns.

Page 226226

Copyright Eastwood Harris Pty Ltd 2020

226

EASTWOOD HARRIS PTY LTD.

Assigning a Code to a Single Task

- To assign a code to a single task,
  - Place the cursor on the code in the **Project View**,
  - Left click and drag to the task bar in the Gantt Chart,
  - You may receive the following message,

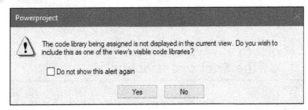

Powerproject

⚠ The code library being assigned is not displayed in the current view. Do you wish to include this as one of the view's visible code libraries?

☐ Do not show this alert again

| Yes | No |

  - Click **Yes** to apply the new **Code Library** formatting to all the task bars.

EASTWOOD HARRIS PTY LTD.

Assigning a Code to a Multiple Tasks

- To assign a code to a multiple tasks,
  - Select multiple task bars in the Gantt Chart or Line No by Crtl clicking,
  - Place the cursor on the code in the **Project View**,
  - Left click and drag the Code Value on to one of the task bars in the Gantt Chart,
  - You may receive the following message,

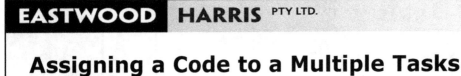

Powerproject

⚠ The code library being assigned is not displayed in the current view. Do you wish to include this as one of the view's visible code libraries?

☐ Do not show this alert again

| Yes | No |

  - Click **Yes** to apply the new Code Library colour to all the task bars.

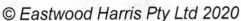

EASTWOOD HARRIS PTY LTD.

Selecting which code is displayed on task bars

- When one **Code Library** is to be used to format the tasks,

- From the **Project View**,

    - Select the **Code Library** :

    - Right Click on the Code Library heading and select **Display Library**,

    - The red tick identifies the code library used to colour tasks,

- Version 14 and earlier only allowed on Code Library to be displayed on tasks,

- In Version 15 if any other Code Libraries have a red tick this needs to be removed using the same process so only one Code Library has a red tick.

EASTWOOD HARRIS PTY LTD.

Open Code Breakdown Structure Command

To quickly view your tasks under their Codes:

- Right click on the **Code Library** heading and

- Select **Open Code Breakdown Structure**:

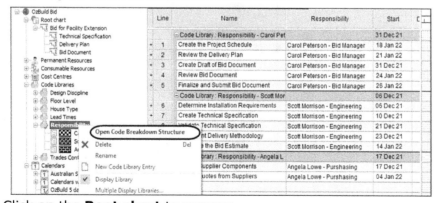

- Click on the **Root chart** to remove.

EASTWOOD HARRIS PTY LTD.

Multiple Display Libraries

- A new function in Powerproject Version 15 allows the formatting of bars to be read from multiple Codes Libraries using the **Multiple Display Libraries** option,

- When more than one Code Library has been assigned to a task:

  - Only one Code Library will be displayed on the bar,

  - The colouring from the Code highest in the list in the **Multiple Display Libraries** form is displayed on the bar.

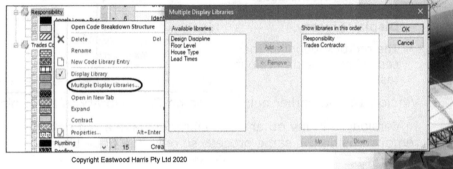

231

EASTWOOD HARRIS PTY LTD.

Introduction to filters...

- Now that the project is coded, filters may be used to show only the tasks with a certain code,

- To filter on a code:

  - Select the **View** tab, **View Data** group, **Filter**, and

  - Select a Code Based filter that may be named differently to the picture:

232

EASTWOOD HARRIS PTY LTD.

Introduction to filters

- Click on the + against the required code to display the available codes,

- Check the required values,

- Click on **Finish** to run the filter,

- Select **View**, **Filter**, **No Filter** to remove the filter.

Filter Wizard - Code library for Which Code? [asks for a code(s)]

Which code library entries do you wish to appear in your filter?
Only objects which have one or more of the codes selected will appear in your filtered view.

- Code Library
  - Design Discipline
  - Floor Level
  - House Type
  - Lead Times
  - Responsibility
    - no codes
    - Angela Lowe - Purchasing
    - Carol Peterson - Bid Manager
    - Scott Morrison - Engineering
  - Trades Contractor

- ● Look for bar or task codes
- ○ Look for task codes only
- ○ Look for bar codes only
- ○ Look for allocation codes only

☑ Ask me which code library entries to use each time the filter is applied

< Back   Next >   Finish   Cancel   Help

Copyright Eastwood Harris Pty Ltd 2020

233

EASTWOOD HARRIS PTY LTD.

10 – CODE LIBRARIES – SUMMARY

In this module we covered:

- Creating Code Libraries,

- Assigning Codes to Tasks,

- Selecting which code is displayed on task bars,

- Introduction to filters.

Copyright Eastwood Harris Pty Ltd 2020

234

EASTWOOD **HARRIS** PTY LTD.

Workshop 10 – Code Libraries

- We want to issue reports for comment by management by assigning responsibility to the activities, and

- Then applying filters for each responsible person.

EASTWOOD **HARRIS** PTY LTD.

11 - FILTERS

In this module we will cover:

- Understanding Filters
- Applying a Filter
- Filtering using the Root Chart
- Creating a New Filter.

Understanding Filters

- Powerproject has an ability to display tasks that meet specific criteria using filters,

- Powerproject defaults to displaying all tasks,

- Templates may include a number of predefined filters that you may use or edit and you may also create one or more of your own,

- Interactive filters may be created and may be customised when applied. For example a filter may be created to select a code value and the value is selected from a list when the filter applied. This works in a similar way to a Microsoft Interactive Filter,

- The **Filter Wizard** designed to create filters but is difficult to use,

- The simplest way to create a new filter is to copy an existing filter with similar parameters and edit it.

Copyright Eastwood Harris Pty Ltd 2020

237

Understanding Filters

- Filters may be viewed in the filter menu or **Library Explorer**,

- Filters may be assigned a **Filter Category** and then they are displayed in a **Filter** submenu,

- Filters may also be hidden from all menus and only displayed in the **More Filter Menu** when **Display** on menu is not checked,

- These attributes may be seen in the **Library Explorer**:

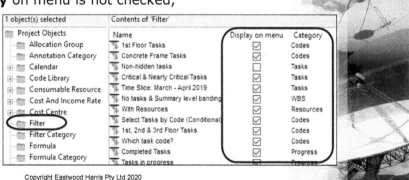

Copyright Eastwood Harris Pty Ltd 2020

238

117

Applying an Existing Filter

- Filters are displayed in the main **Filter Menu** when they are not assigned a **Filter Category** or

- Displayed in a **Submenu** when assigned a **Filter Category**:

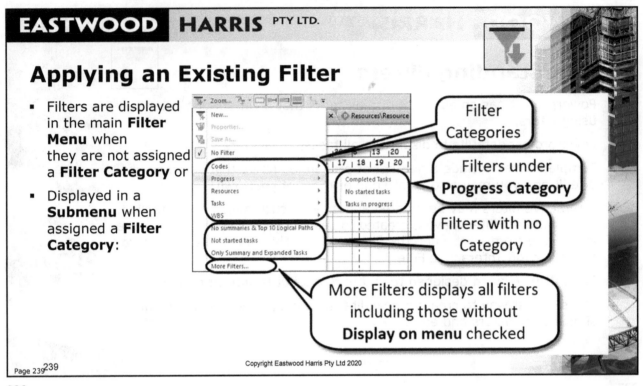

Filter Categories

Filters under **Progress Category**

Filters with no Category

More Filters displays all filters including those without **Display on menu** checked

Page 239²³⁹

239

Filtering using the Root Chart

- Often it is simpler to reduce the number of tasks in view by selecting the appropriate nodes in the **Root Chart**,

- This may be only completed when **Summary Tasks** are used and not when tasks are grouped by WBS or Code,

- The picture below shows only the tasks under the two selected **Summary Tasks**:

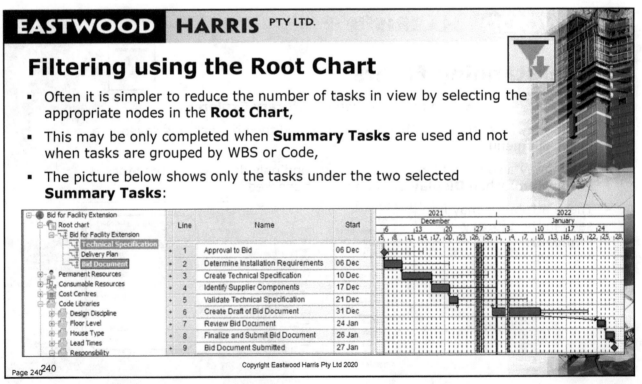

Page 240²⁴⁰

240

EASTWOOD **HARRIS** PTY LTD.

Creating a New Filter

- There are two ways of creating a new filter:
  - Select **View**, **Filter**, **New:** and use the **Filter Wizard** to create a new filter, or
  - **Copy** an existing one using the **Save As** function,
- The **Filter Wizard** is complex and has many dialogue boxes that are not simple to master,
- Often it is simpler to copy an existing filter that is similar to the one you require and edit it,
- **Note:** You may also open another project and copy and paste a filter from another project using **Library Explorer**.

241

EASTWOOD **HARRIS** PTY LTD.

Creating a New Filter using the Filter Wizard...

- To create a new filter select **View**, **Filter**, **New**,
- Assign the filter a **Name**,
- To add the filter to the **Menu** select **Display on menu**,
- Assign a **Category** if required,
- Multiple **Criteria** are allowed and select **Insert** to insert a second Criteria line,
- Complete the **Criteria logic** and **Filter options**,
- **Subheading properties** allows a hierarchy of summary tasks to be concatenated on one line,
- Select **Edit** to edit the selected criteria filter.

242

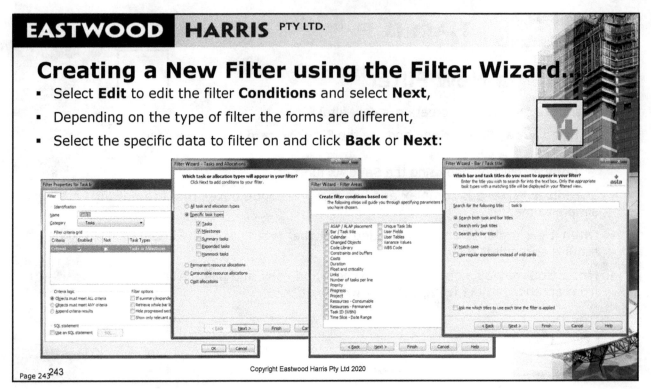

EASTWOOD HARRIS PTY LTD.

Creating a New Filter using the Filter Wizard...

- Select **Edit** to edit the filter **Conditions** and select **Next**,
- Depending on the type of filter the forms are different,
- Select the specific data to filter on and click **Back** or **Next**:

Page 243
243

Copyright Eastwood Harris Pty Ltd 2020

243

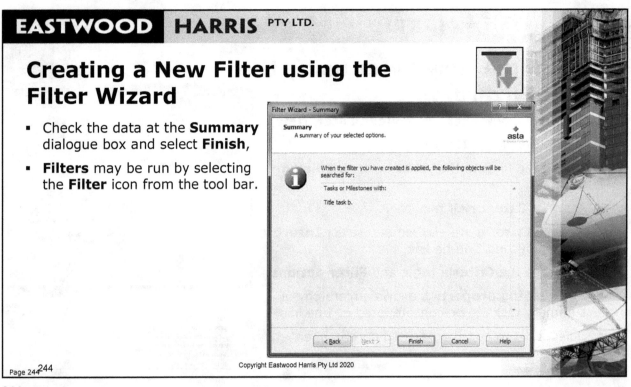

EASTWOOD HARRIS PTY LTD.

Creating a New Filter using the Filter Wizard

- Check the data at the **Summary** dialogue box and select **Finish**,
- **Filters** may be run by selecting the **Filter** icon from the tool bar.

Page 244
244

Copyright Eastwood Harris Pty Ltd 2020

244

120

EASTWOOD HARRIS PTY LTD.

11 – FILTERS - SUMMARY

In this module we covered:

- Understanding Filters
- Applying a Filter
- Filtering using the Root Chart
- Creating a New Filter.

Copyright Eastwood Harris Pty Ltd 2020

245

EASTWOOD HARRIS PTY LTD.

Workshop 11 - Filters

- In this workshop we will apply some existing filters.

Copyright Eastwood Harris Pty Ltd 2020

246

EASTWOOD HARRIS PTY LTD.

12 – ORGANISING TASKS USING SORT AND GROUP

- Powerproject may Sort and Group tasks on Codes and other project parameters in the same way as P6 or Microsoft Project,

- This function is used to group tasks by Codes such as trade, floor, area, responsibility, contractor etc, or by other parameters such as the Task Calendar or Float,

- This module will show you how to create and apply a **Sort and Group**,

- The **Sort/Group Properties** form is used to create new **Sort and Group** has may options and takes a little time to understand,

- A **Sort and Group** is applied to and save with a **View**,

- Often the simplest way to create a new **Sort and Group** is to copy an existing one with similar parameters and edit it.

Page 247 247

247

EASTWOOD HARRIS PTY LTD.

Creating a Sort and Group...

- The **Sort and Group** to be demonstrated in this module will use the Responsibility Code library,

- Select **View**, **Sort/Group**,

- Select **New...**, to open the **Sort/Group Properties** form,

- Assign a name for the sort, e.g. **By Responsibility**,

- Select a **Category** if required,

- Check **Display on menu** if you want the **Group/Sort** displayed in the menu.

Page 248 248

248

Creating a Sort and Group...

- Select the object type that you wish to sort on in the **Type** column, this is typically **Task**,
- Select the data to sort by in the **Attribute** column,
- The picture shows Responsibility has been selected,
- Select the direction of the sort in the Direction drop down.

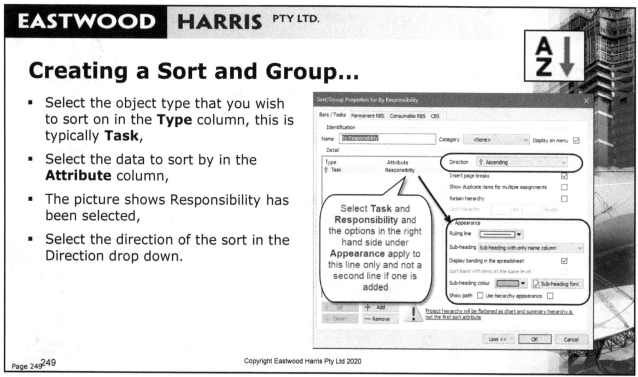

Creating a Sort...

- Select **Insert page break** to place page break at the bottom of each data set to print each group of data on a new page,
- Check the other options as required,
- The **Sub-heading** drop down formats the summary heading,
- The text font and band colouring may be formatted,
- Click **OK** to apply the sort

Creating a Sort...

- The simple **Group and Sort** demonstrated will give the result as per below:

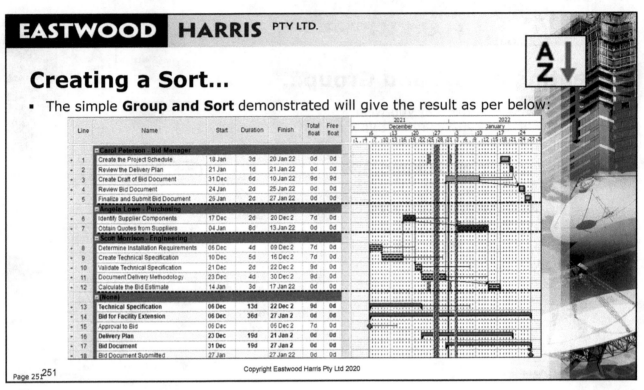

Creating a Sort and Group...

- If you want the activities ordered in a specific way you may add a second line to sort the tasks,

- The picture below displays the task sorted alphabetically:

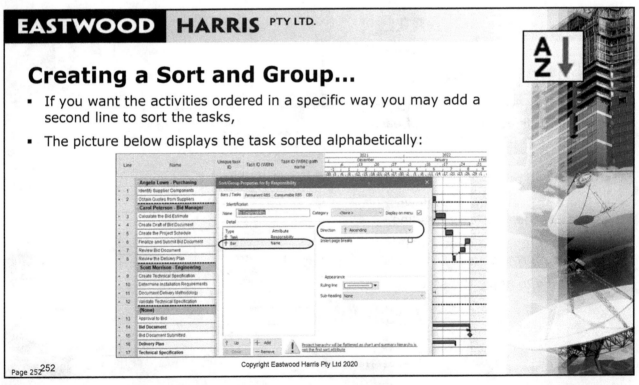

EASTWOOD HARRIS PTY LTD.

Creating a Sort and Group

- Tasks may be grouped by a second band,
- The picture below displays the task Grouped by Responsibility and Calendar::

Page 253 253

Copyright Eastwood Harris Pty Ltd 2020

253

EASTWOOD HARRIS PTY LTD.

Creating a Sort and Group

- **Project Hierarchy** is by default the first line and when this is removed then the **Task-per-line function** is disabled,
- When **Project Hierarchy** is left as the first line then activities are first Grouped by the Summary Tasks first.

Page 254 254

254

Removing a Group and Sort

- Selecting **Natural Order** from the **Group/Sort** menu will remove all Grouping and Sorting,

- This option will then sort the tasks by the outlined summary tasks,

- Selecting **Natural Order** is the same as having a **Group/Sort** by **Project Hierarchy** only.

Copyright Eastwood Harris Pty Ltd 2020

255

---

12 – ORGANISING TASKS USING SORT AND GROUP - SUMMARY

In this module we have covered how to:

- Create and apply a **Sort and Group** and

- Remove a **Sort and Group**.

Copyright Eastwood Harris Pty Ltd 2020

256

EASTWOOD HARRIS PTY LTD.

Workshop 12 - Organizing Tasks using Sort and Group

- You will create a **Sort and Group** to group the tasks by Responsibility.

Copyright Eastwood Harris Pty Ltd 2020

257

EASTWOOD HARRIS PTY LTD.

13 - PRINTING & REPORTS

There are some tools available to output your schedule to a printer and produce reports:

- The **Printing** function prints the data displayed in the current View,

- You may wish to create views that are used just for printing, so you do not mess them up while creating and updating your program,

- **Powerdraw** is used to edit your **Border files** for formatting your printout borders, this enables borders to be created so they are in proportion to your paper,

- The **Reporting** function prints reports or export reports to Excel, which are independent of the current View,

- Powerproject supplies a number of predefined reports that may be tailored to suit your own requirements.

Copyright Eastwood Harris Pty Ltd 2020

258

EASTWOOD HARRIS PTY LTD.

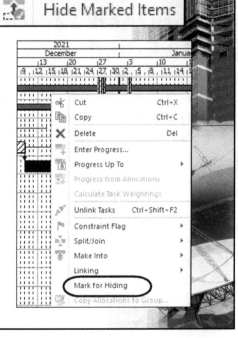

Hiding Tasks before Printing...

- Sometimes you may wish to temporarily hide some tasks before printing,
- This is similar to filtering but the tasks do not have to meet a criteria,
- In order to hide specific tasks, you must first mark them for hiding, and then hide them:
  - Select one or more the task bars in the Gantt Chart,
  - Right click and select **Mark For Hiding** from the menu that appears or click on the Quick Access Toolbar button after it has been added,
  - Once you have marked items you may hide or display them from view at any time by clicking the **Hide Marked Items** button when added to a toolbar.

EASTWOOD HARRIS PTY LTD.

Hide Marked Items

Hiding Tasks before Printing

- To Show Hidden tasks:
  - When tasks are hidden, the **Hide Marked Items** toolbar button changes to have a highlighted background,
  - The **Hide Marked Items** toolbar button may be clicked at any time to restore the hidden tasks,
- To unmark the tasks so they are not hidden in future:
  - Select the task,
  - Right click in the Gantt Chart and select **Mark for Hiding** again to unmark the tasks,
- The **Mark for hiding** column may be displayed to identify which tasks are marked and to mark tasks,
- **Note:** The **Show/Hide** button from Version 14 has disappeared in Version 15.

Understanding Powerdraw and Border Files

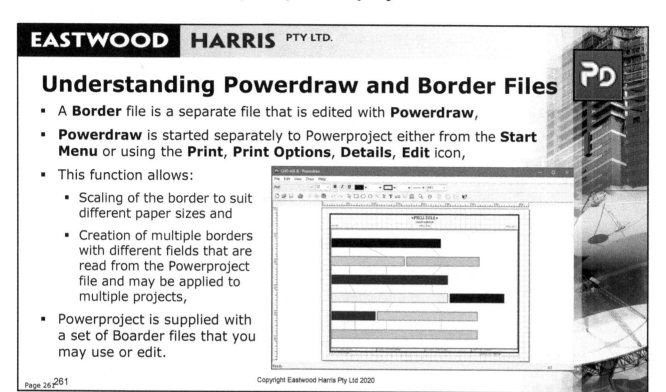

- A **Border** file is a separate file that is edited with **Powerdraw**,

- **Powerdraw** is started separately to Powerproject either from the **Start Menu** or using the **Print**, **Print Options**, **Details**, **Edit** icon,

- This function allows:
  - Scaling of the border to suit different paper sizes and
  - Creation of multiple borders with different fields that are read from the Powerproject file and may be applied to multiple projects,

- Powerproject is supplied with a set of Boarder files that you may use or edit.

261

Printing the Project

- Select **File**, **Print** or select the **Print** button,

- **Print Now** will print the project with the existing options,

- **Print Options** allows you to format the printout,

- **Full Preview** uses the whole screen for preview and access to formatting commands through a toolbar.

262

EASTWOOD HARRIS PTY LTD.

Print Options, Output - Understanding Clipboard and Picture File

- **Printer** is self explanatory,

- **Clipboard** is where Powerproject takes a 'snap shot' of your project and then you may paste it into another program from the Clipboard,

- **Picture File** is similar to the clipboard option:

  - But instead of storing it in the computers memory it writes it as a picture file (JPEG extension),

  - Thus you may either email it or insert it as a picture object in another application such as MS Word, PowerPoint, Excel or Outlook.

263

EASTWOOD HARRIS PTY LTD.

Print Options, Details

- Select **Browse...** from the **Details** tab and select your border file,

- Then select the orientation and page size,

- **Date Range**,

- **Embed** saves the border as part of the project file,

- The current print options may be saved as a **Print profile** and then applied to other projects.

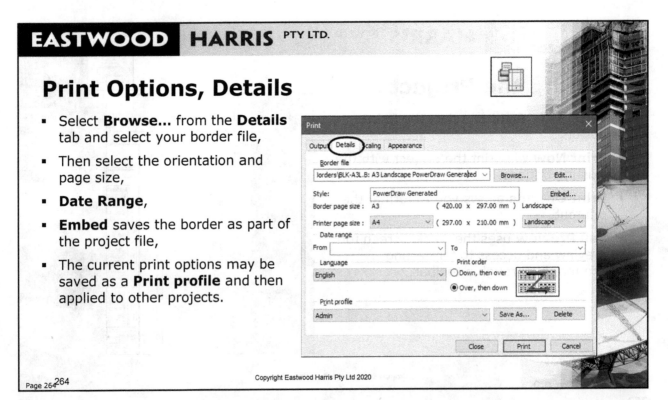

264

Create and Update an Unresourced Project Using Elecosoft (Asta) Powerproject Version 15.2

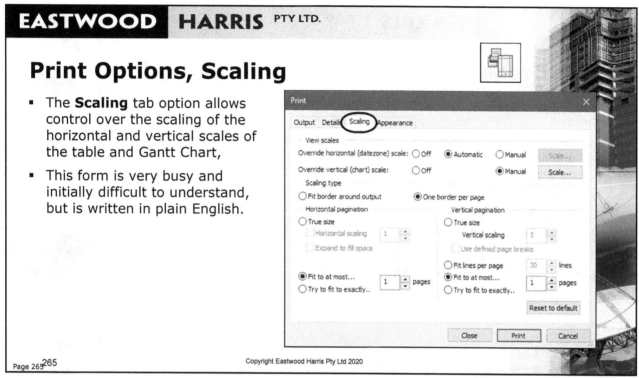

Print Options, Scaling

- The **Scaling** tab option allows control over the scaling of the horizontal and vertical scales of the table and Gantt Chart,

- This form is very busy and initially difficult to understand, but is written in plain English.

265

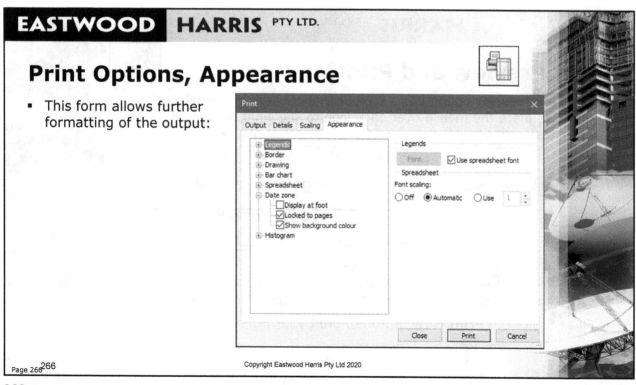

Print Options, Appearance

- This form allows further formatting of the output:

266

131

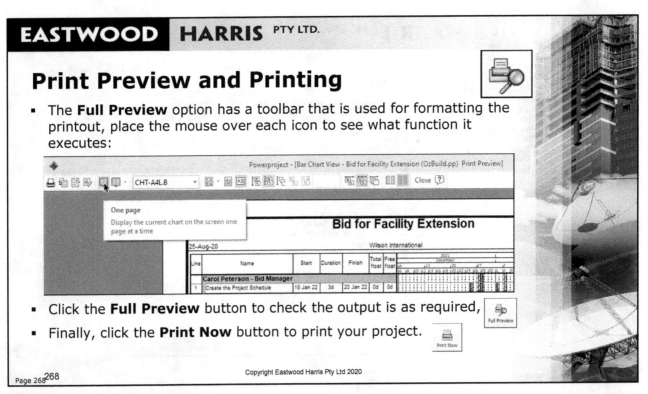

EASTWOOD HARRIS PTY LTD.

Reports

- Powerproject has many inbuilt tabular reports that may be exported in many formats,
- These are typically exported in to Excel for formatting and presentation purposes.

Copyright Eastwood Harris Pty Ltd 2020

269

EASTWOOD HARRIS PTY LTD.

Tabular Reports

- To produce a tabular report:
  - Select the **Project**, **Data**, **Reports** to open the **Reports** menu,
  - Choose the category and the report you wish to run:

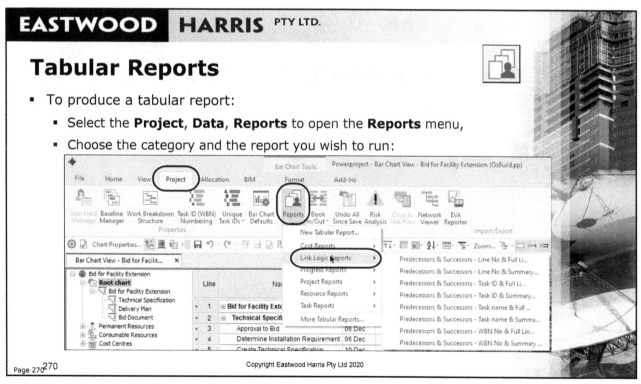

Copyright Eastwood Harris Pty Ltd 2020

270

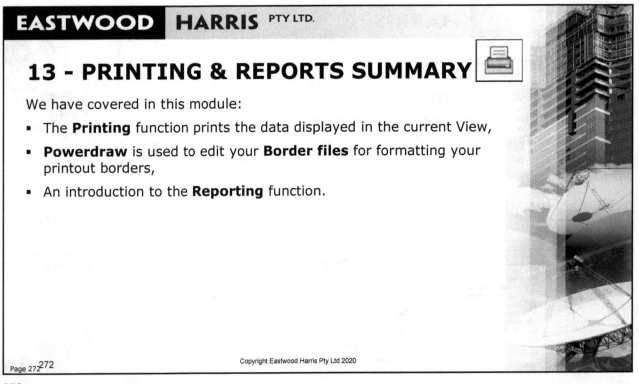

EASTWOOD HARRIS PTY LTD.

Tabular Reports...

- Tabular Reports are specified in the **Report Properties** form which is opened from the **Reports, More Tabular Reports...**, then select the report and click on **Properties**,

- This form also specifies where the report is run in the **Output** tab.

Copyright Eastwood Harris Pty Ltd 2020

EASTWOOD HARRIS PTY LTD.

13 - PRINTING & REPORTS SUMMARY

We have covered in this module:

- The **Printing** function prints the data displayed in the current View,

- **Powerdraw** is used to edit your **Border files** for formatting your printout borders,

- An introduction to the **Reporting** function.

Copyright Eastwood Harris Pty Ltd 2020

EASTWOOD HARRIS PTY LTD.

Workshop 13 - Printing

- You will print your project.

273

EASTWOOD HARRIS PTY LTD.

14 – BASELINES

- A Baseline is a software function used to record the project status at a particular point in time allowing comparison of project progress at different stages,

- Baselines may be used to:

  - Compare progress with an agreed contract plan, or

  - Compare one periods' progress with another, in order to evaluate slippage etc., or

  - For claims analysis, with the Baseline recording the status before a delay or acceleration is applied to the Live schedule,

- A Baseline may record all or some activities and includes all task data such as bars, tasks, links, resource/cost allocations, libraries, histograms and annotations,

- Unlike P6, part projects in Powerproject may be baselined,

- Microsoft Project does not Baseline logic, constraints or the critical path.

274

EASTWOOD HARRIS PTY LTD.

Powerproject Version 15 Baseline functionality changes

- In earlier versions of Powerproject a baseline was saved as a separate file with a *.ppb file extension,

- In Version 15.1 baselines are saved as part of the Live (current) project file which is in *.pp format. Thus a single *.pp file will contain the current project data and all baselines making sharing a complete project simpler as you only have to share one file,

- Version 15.2 introduced to option of keeping baseline files separate as in earlier versions of Powerproject,

- You may export the baseline to a separate *.pp file to supply a person with a copy of a Baseline or to make a *.pp file smaller,

- You may import a baseline and specify how to map the imported tasks to the current project tasks,

- You may also import Primavera XER file as a baseline.

Copyright Eastwood Harris Pty Ltd 2020

EASTWOOD HARRIS PTY LTD.

Creating Baselines...

To create a Baseline:

- Select relevant tasks to set a partial baseline,

- Select **Project**, **Properties**, **Baseline Manager** to open the **Baseline/What If Manager** form,

- Click **New** to run the **Baseline Wizard**:

[Baseline/What If Manager (Bid for Facility Extension) dialog showing columns: Name, ID, Created, Updated, Active, Current, Imported, Deleted, Reverting To with "There are no items to show." and buttons New, Merge, Delete, Set As Current, Revert To, Import, Export. Details section with Pathname, Description, Appearance fields and Revert Options: Restore deleted objects, Restore deleted and changed objects, Restore selected objects, Overwrite. Close, Cancel, Apply buttons.]

Copyright Eastwood Harris Pty Ltd 2020

EASTWOOD HARRIS PTY LTD.

Creating Baselines...

- Enter the baseline **Name** and **Description** in the **Details** form and select **Next**,
- **Embed the baseline in the file** decides if a separate Baseline file is created,
- The **Destination** form is only displayed when the Baseline is not embedded,
- Complete the **Scope** form and select **Next**,
- Check the details in **Summary** and select **Finish** to save the Baseline:

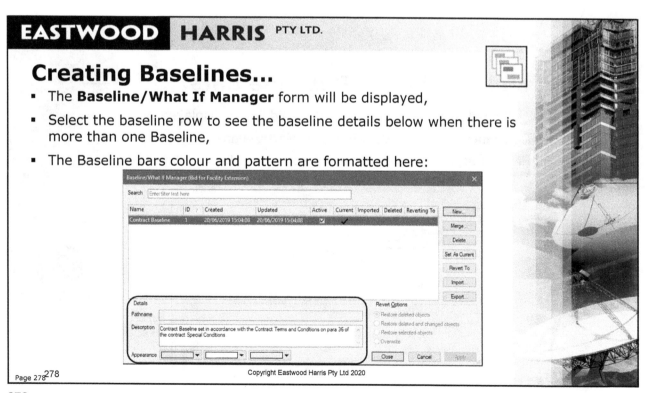

Copyright Eastwood Harris Pty Ltd 2020

277

EASTWOOD HARRIS PTY LTD.

Creating Baselines...

- The **Baseline/What If Manager** form will be displayed,
- Select the baseline row to see the baseline details below when there is more than one Baseline,
- The Baseline bars colour and pattern are formatted here:

Copyright Eastwood Harris Pty Ltd 2020

278

EASTWOOD HARRIS PTY LTD.

Creating Baselines

- This baseline has a tick under the **Current** heading,
- When there are multiple Baselines one only may be checked as **Current** which allows you to change the **Current Baseline** in the **Baseline/What if Manager** form,
- All reports that refer to the **Current Baseline** will be adjusted accordingly,
- This is a very useful feature when you wish to show the last period baseline in your reports and you just have to change the Current Baseline in one place and not have to change lots of Views.

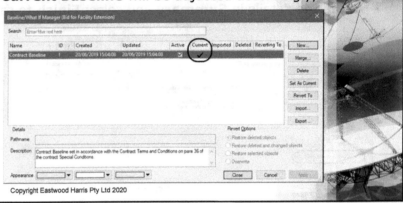

Page 279 279

Copyright Eastwood Harris Pty Ltd 2020

279

EASTWOOD HARRIS PTY LTD.

Hiding and Displaying Baseline Bars

- Each View will need to have the Baseline Bars hidden or displayed by either:
  - From the **Format Bar Chart**, **Baseline** tab select the one you wish to display, or
  - Select the **Format**, **Show/Hide** baselines icon which hides displayed Baselines:

Page 280 280

280

EASTWOOD HARRIS PTY LTD.

Revert and Merging a Baseline

- Use the **Revert** function to convert a Baseline file into the Live (Current) Project, click with care,

- **Merging** a Baseline brings in missing data from a Live Project into the Baseline, again use with care,

- Before using either the **Revert** and **Merging** functions take a copy of your programme.

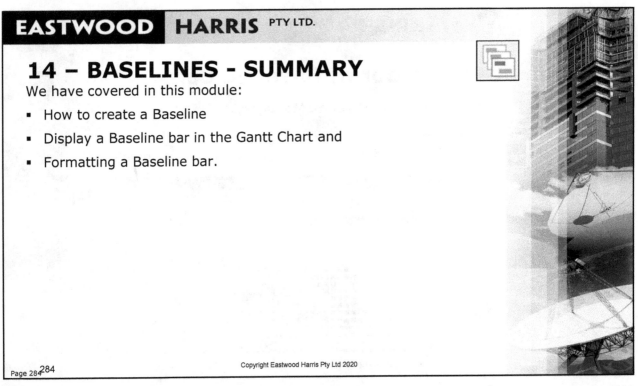

Copyright Eastwood Harris Pty Ltd 2020

Page 283

283

EASTWOOD HARRIS PTY LTD.

14 – BASELINES - SUMMARY

We have covered in this module:

- How to create a Baseline
- Display a Baseline bar in the Gantt Chart and
- Formatting a Baseline bar.

Copyright Eastwood Harris Pty Ltd 2020

Page 284

284

EASTWOOD HARRIS PTY LTD.

Workshop 14 – Setting the Baseline

- The project has been approved and you will need to set a baseline.

Copyright Eastwood Harris Pty Ltd 2020

285

EASTWOOD HARRIS PTY LTD.

15 - UPDATING AN UNRESOURCED PROJECT

This module will cover the following topics:

- Concepts for Updating an Unresourced Project
- Multiple Reports Dates
- Displaying Progress
- Progress Options and Setting the Progress Date
- Understanding the Percent Complete fields
- Entering Progress
- Overall Percent Complete Weighting
- Task Work
- Rescheduling with Progress
- Workshop 15 - Updating the Schedule and Baseline Comparison.

Copyright Eastwood Harris Pty Ltd 2020

286

EASTWOOD HARRIS PTY LTD.

Updating an Unresourced Project

- The are many methods of updating progress and Powerproject has far more options than most competitors and some that are complex to understand,

- It is suggested that you decide what results you are seeking and then work out the options you require before you update your schedule,

- Document the **Options** and test them on a simple schedule,

- Then apply them to your working schedule,

- Organisations should create procedures and templates with all the **Schedule Options** set to simplify the setting up of project programmes for less experienced users,

- **NOTE:** It is generally accepted that a properly updated schedule will have all the completed work in the past with Actual Dates representing when the work was performed and all incomplete work in the future. This schedule would then provide a revised project finish date.

EASTWOOD HARRIS PTY LTD.

Updating an Unresourced Project

There are two main methods used with Powerproject to update a schedule:

- The first method is to just enter the **Percent Complete** against each task which will show if activities are ahead or behind of the **Report Date**,

  - This does not reschedule incomplete work that is scheduled in the past forward in time into the future, or reschedule complete work scheduled in the future back to the past, both of these situations are illogical, and

  - This leaves a **Jagged Report Line**, and **NOT** considered a properly updated schedule,

- The second method is to **Straighten the Report Line** which reschedules:

  - Incomplete work into the future based on the logic and remaining durations, and

  - Moves complete work into the past, thus Actual Dates may not be correct but theses may be adjusted to produce a properly updated program,

- **NOTE:** P6 only updates a schedule with a **Straight Report Line** and this may be set as the default in Powerproject and the **Jagged Report Line** not used.

Updating An Unresourced Project

- This module will look at two methods of updating a program with Powerproject.
- The main steps for monitoring progress are:
  - Set the **Reschedule Options** to reflect how you wish to update your schedule,
  - Saving a **Baseline** schedule, covered in the last module,
  - Record or mark-up progress as of a specific date, know in Powerproject as the **Report Date**,
  - Update the schedule,
  - Straightening the **Progress Line**, forcing all incomplete work into the future and incomplete work into the past,
  - Comparing and reporting actual progress against planned progress and revising the plan and schedule, as required.

Understanding the Concepts

There are three stages in a task lifecycle:

- **Not Started** – The Early Start and Early Finish dates are calculated from the Predecessors, Constraints, and Task Duration,
- **In-Progress** – The task has an Actual Start date but is not complete:
  - The task is assigned an Actual Start date, normally entered in the past in relationship to the Report Date, which will override the Start Constraints and Start links that were originally used to calculate the Early Start,
  - The Finish Date will be calculated from the Report Date and the Remaining Duration,
- **Complete** – The task is in the past, the Actual Start and Actual Finish dates are manually entered in the past and they override all logic and constraints.

Understanding Multiple Report Dates and Progress Periods

- Microsoft Project, P6 and many other scheduling software packages have one **Data Date** (P6 term) or **Status Date** (Microsoft Project term) that is moved forward in time each time a project schedule is updated,

- Powerproject allows the creation of multiple **Report Dates** and then you have a choice of either using:

  - One **Project Report Date** which may be displayed and moved forward in time as the project progresses. This is the process P6 and Microsoft Project use, or

  - Multiple **Project Report Dates** which creates **Progress Periods** between pairs of **Project Report Dates**. This will in turn enable the display the progress in each **Progress Period**.

Creating Multiple Progress Periods

To create multiple **Report Dates** which in turn creates multiple **Progress Periods**:

- Open the **Library Explorer**,

- Select **Progress Period**,

- There will normally be at least one date and you may rename it, then

- Add additional **Report Dates** every week or month to reflect when you plan to update your schedule:

	1 object(s) selected		Contents of 'Progress Period'		
	Project Objects		Name	Report date	Line style
	Calendar		Project Report Date	06-Dec-21 00:00	
	Code Library				
	Cost And Income Rate				
	Cost Centre				
	Consumable Resource				
	Currency Unit				
	Exception				
	Filter				
	Link Category				
	Permanent Resource				
	Progress Period				
	Resource Report				

Name	Report date	Line style
Week 1	13/12/2021 00:00	
Week 2	20/12/2021 00:00	
Week 3	27/12/2021 00:00	
Week 4	3/01/2022 00:00	
Week 5	10/01/2022 00:00	
Week 6	17/01/2022 00:00	
Week 7	24/01/2022 00:00	
Week 8	31/01/2022 00:00	

EASTWOOD HARRIS PTY LTD.

Setting the Progress Entry Period Date

- When multiple **Progress Periods** are created only one may be set as the **Progress Entry Period** for the update you are about to enter,

- The current **Progress Period** has a red tick against it in the **Project View** and may be set by either:

  - In the **Project View** right click and select **Progress Entry Period** or

  - In the **Reschedule Progress Period Warning** form,

- **NOTE:** There are two date fields in the **Reschedule Progress Period Warning** form and it is best to keep them the same by setting the **Straighten progress period** to **Progress entry period**.

Page 293

293

EASTWOOD HARRIS PTY LTD.

Displaying Progress Periods on the Gantt Chart

To view the progress lines:

- Open the **Format Bar Chart** form, **Progress** tab,

- Check the **Lines On** check box to display **Progress Lines**,

- Check the boxes for **Progress Lines** you wish to display,

- **Line style** allows a:

  - **Jagged Progress Line** or

  - **Straight Progress Line** or

  - **Straight Progress Line on Summaries/Hammocks** is used with the **Jagged Line** option but is Straight on Hammocks and Summaries,

  - The picture displays a **Jagged Progress Line**:

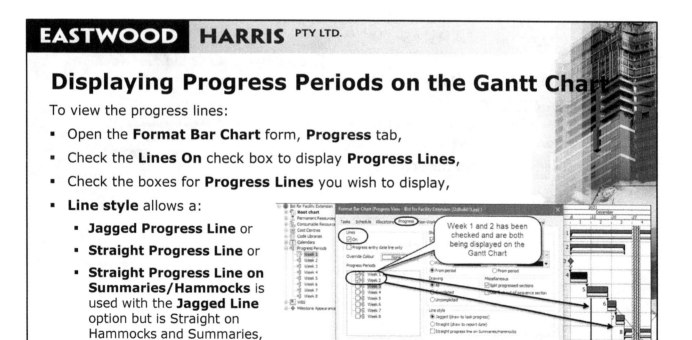

Page 294

294

EASTWOOD HARRIS PTY LTD.

Displaying Progress Periods on the Gantt Chart

- If you check the **Progress entry line date only** option, Powerproject will only show the **Report Date** line of the selected **Progress Entry Period** selected in the Project View and not display any other Progress Lines:

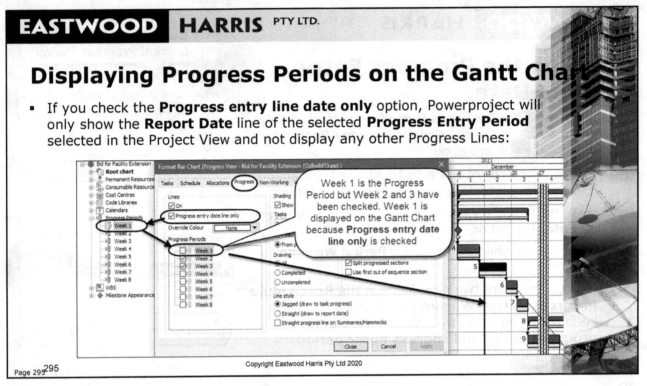

Week 1 is the Progress Period but Week 2 and 3 have been checked. Week 1 is displayed on the Gantt Chart because **Progress entry date line only** is checked

EASTWOOD HARRIS PTY LTD.

Displaying progress in the bar chart

Before we assign progress you need to ensure that progress will be displayed,

- **Show Shading** displays the progress shading,

- **Default shading** shades half of the bar and

- **Solid shading** shades the whole bar,

- **Fixed Shading** shades progress for each period in the colour selected and

- **From Period** shades the progress for each period in the same colour as the **Progress Period Line** for the period progress was recorded.

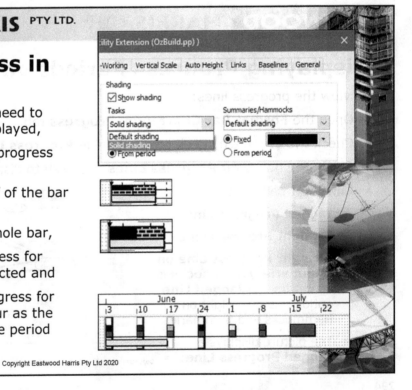

EASTWOOD HARRIS PTY LTD.

Progress Options...

- Before entering progress you must check your **Progress Options**,

- Select **File**, **Options**,

- Select the **Progress** tab,

- **Snapping** is very useful as you are able to keep the Duration Remaining to round days and in turn one day tasks do not start in the middle of the day and span two days,

- The defaults are usually good and should not be changed unless they are well understood,

- See the **Powerproject Help** for details.

Options for Bid for Facility Extension

Edit   Assign   View   Format   **Progress**   Reschedule   File Locations   Calendars   Spreadsheet   General

Progress entry mode
- ◉ Update duration in step
- ○ Fill to progress line
- ☐ Do not recompute remaining after overall percent update

Snapping
- ☑ Snap actual/remaining duration to snapping unit

Progress snapping unit   ⊙ Days   ⌄

Jagged Progress View
- ◉ Use current baseline
- ○ Use project baseline(s)

Ribbon, toolbar progress controls and percent complete field
- ◉ Duration percent complete
- ○ Overall percent complete

Miscellaneous
- ☐ Enter progress shows 'User Percent Complete'
- ☐ In Progress from allocations, recalculate durations where allocation is calculated
- ☐ Update progress via duration remaining

Progress method   Duration - Approximate   ⌄
Site Progress Login   Company ID and Username   ⌄

Close

EASTWOOD HARRIS PTY LTD.

Progress Options...

- Under **Progress Entry Mode** decide if you would like to:

  - **Update duration in step**, or

  - **Fill to progress line**, this is similar to the way P6 calculates:

  - **Fill to progress line** with **Do not recomputed remaining after overall percent complete**:

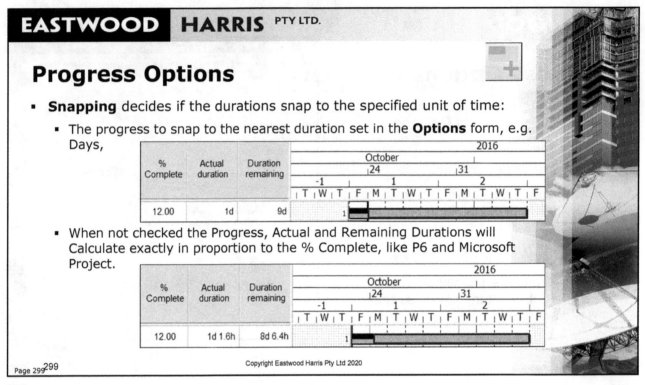

Progress Options

- **Snapping** decides if the durations snap to the specified unit of time:
  - The progress to snap to the nearest duration set in the **Options** form, e.g. Days,

% Complete	Actual duration	Duration remaining	October 2016
12.00	1d	9d	

  - When not checked the Progress, Actual and Remaining Durations will Calculate exactly in proportion to the % Complete, like P6 and Microsoft Project.

% Complete	Actual duration	Duration remaining	October 2016
12.00	1d 1.6h	8d 6.4h	

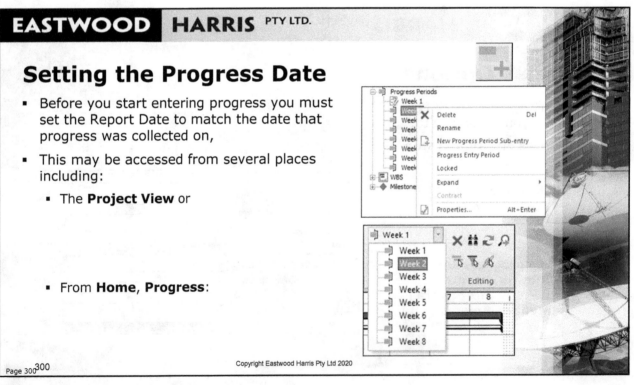

Setting the Progress Date

- Before you start entering progress you must set the Report Date to match the date that progress was collected on,
- This may be accessed from several places including:
  - The **Project View** or
  - From **Home**, **Progress**:

148

EASTWOOD HARRIS PTY LTD.

Understanding the Percent Complete fields

- Duration = Actual duration + Duration remaining,
- The Percent Complete = Actual duration/Duration,
- A change to the Duration will change the Duration remaining,
- When a task is updated using either the **Duration remaining** or **Percent Complete** the **Overall Percent Complete** is also updated to be the same value,
- The **Overall Percent Complete** may be edited afterwards without changing the **Duration remaining** or **Percent Complete**,
- The **Overall Percent Complete** may be assigned a **Overall percent weighting** and then Summary Tasks will have a more accurate summary percent complete,
- The **User Percent Complete** is like the P6 and MSP **Physical % Complete** fields may have any value entered and is not linked to any other fields.

301

EASTWOOD HARRIS PTY LTD.

Entering Progress...

- There are several ways to enter progress, including:
  - **Bar and Task Properties** form, **Task**, **Progress** tab,
  - **Bar and Task Properties** view, **Task**, **Progress** tab,
  - Using a **Table** with the appropriate columns,
- To show the progress specific columns you should consider creating a **View** with an associated **Table** that displays the progress columns, has the **Baseline bars** displayed and **Progress Lines** formatted as required.

302

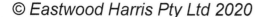

EASTWOOD HARRIS PTY LTD.

Entering Progress

- A progress Table would have the following columns:
    - Line Number and Name
    - Actual Start and Actual Finish
    - Duration, Actual Duration and Duration Remaining
    - Percent Complete
    - Planned Percent Complete (Pointed to the current baseline)
    - Finish variance (Pointed to the current baseline)
- Any progress entered into the Percent Complete column or a Duration column will be displayed on the task bar:

Line	Name	Start	Actual start	Finish	Actual finish	Duration	Actual duration	Duration remaining	User percent complete	Percent complete	Planned % Complete	Finish variance
1	Task	25-Sep-18	25-Sep-18	16-Oct-18		16d	6d	10d	200.00	37.50	50%	-2d

303

EASTWOOD HARRIS PTY LTD.

Overall Percent Complete Weighting...

- One issue with Microsoft Project is that **Summary Task Percent Completes** are calculated from the sum of the **Non Summary Task Actual Durations** divided by the sum of the **Non Summary Task Durations** which in turn leads to misleading Summary task **Actual Durations**, **Remaining Durations** and **% Complete**,
- Also P6 will not give a **Summary % Complete** against **WBS Nodes** when **Physical % Complete** is used,
- The Powerproject **Overall Percent complete** allows a weighting to be assigned to the tasks enabling an accurate user defined **Summary Task % Complete**,
- When tasks are created they are all equally weighted, so when each task is completed an equal amount is shown to have been progressed.

304

EASTWOOD HARRIS PTY LTD.

Overall Percent Complete Weighting

- The first picture shows a summary task with all the Overall percent complete weighting of the sub tasks are the same,

- The second picture shows a summary task with all the Overall percent weighting of the tasks that are different and the Summary Task has a percent complete based on the Overall percent complete weighting of the sub tasks:

305

EASTWOOD **HARRIS** PTY LTD.

Task Work

- The **Task Work** fields allow a task duration to be driven by a **Task Work** and a **Task Work Rate** without resources allocated to tasks,

- The information may be entered in columns or the **Bar and Task Properties** form,

- In Version 15 this may now be displayed in a graph:

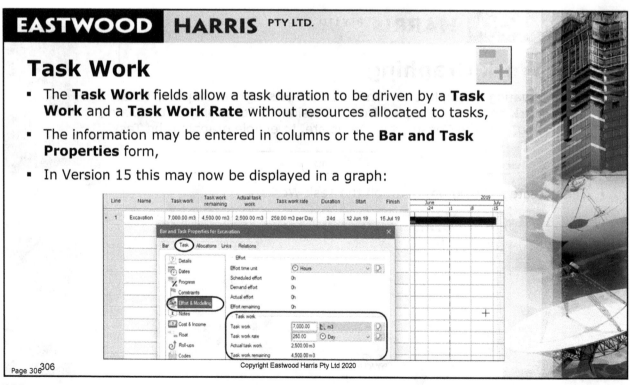

306

EASTWOOD HARRIS PTY LTD.

Task Work Modelling

- The **Options**, **Edit** tab determines whether the **Work Rate** or **Work** is changed when the task duration is changed:

Options for Task Work ✕

Edit Assign View Format Progress Reschedule File Locations Calendars Spreadsheet General

Tasks
When editing start or finish in spreadsheet ○ Change duration ● Move task
When inserting by spreadsheet ● Create subheading ○ Create task
When creating tasks ○ Copy bar name ● Leave name empty
☑ Inherit attributes from neighbouring task ☑ Charts inherit display attributes from parent

Task work
Editing duration for task-work driven task updates ○ Work ● Work rate
Task work rate determiner per

Costs

- This is similar to the P6 resource options of:

  - Fixed Duration and Units = Work

  - Fixed Duration and Units/Time = Work Rate.

EASTWOOD HARRIS PTY LTD.

Task Work Graphing

- When updating a template to Version 15 the **Histogram Report**, **Total Task Work** needs to be copied from a Version 15 Powerproject template Library, such as the Construction Template, to enable graphing the Task Work:

| 📁 Histogram Report | 📊 Total Task Work |

- Then create a Histogram to graph the Task Work:

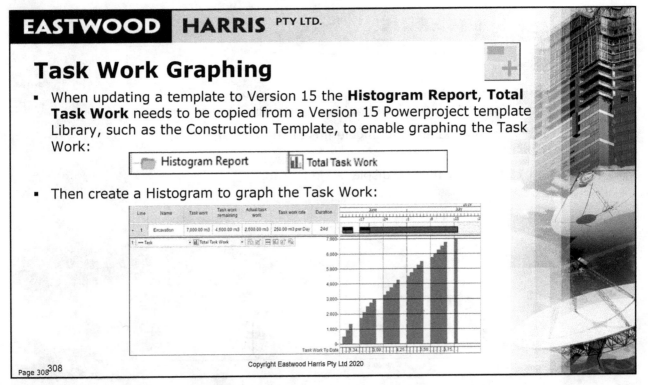

Rescheduling with Progress...

- After progress has been entered the schedule may be rescheduled to straighten the **Report Date** line,

- Select the **Reschedule** command,

- The **Reschedule Progress Period Warning** form will be displayed and the **Straighten progress period** should be set to **Progress entry period**,

- If you do not want to straighten the line, select **None** from the **Straighten progress period** drop down box,

- **NOTE:** If you do not straighten the Progress Line you will not have a properly updated program.

Page 309 309   Copyright Eastwood Harris Pty Ltd 2020

309

Rescheduling with Progress

- Scheduling will straighten **Progress Line** and:
  - Push incomplete portions of tasks into the future and
  - Push completed work into the past:
- **Before** scheduling

- **After** scheduling
- **Note:** Actual Dates will change when a complete part of a task was in the future,
- At this point it would be prudent to ensure the actual dates match when work actually started and finished, especially if your are entering into litigation.

Page 310 310   Copyright Eastwood Harris Pty Ltd 2020

310

EASTWOOD HARRIS PTY LTD.

Jagged Line to Straight Line Display

- If you have followed the update progress over multiple periods and Straightened the Progress Line each time, then you will have a project which will show:
  - The progress for each period, and
  - A revised end date of the project:

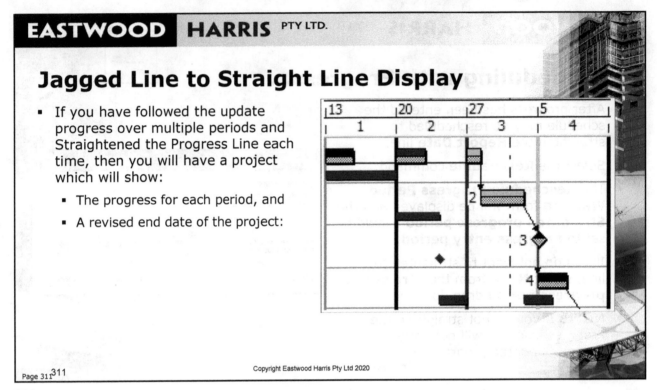

Page 311 311

311

EASTWOOD HARRIS PTY LTD.

Displaying and Editing Period Progress

- As progress is recorded for each period the progress against each task may be displayed on the Gantt Chart,
- Each individual split part of the completed task may be edited by right clicking on the task and selecting the Progress Period :

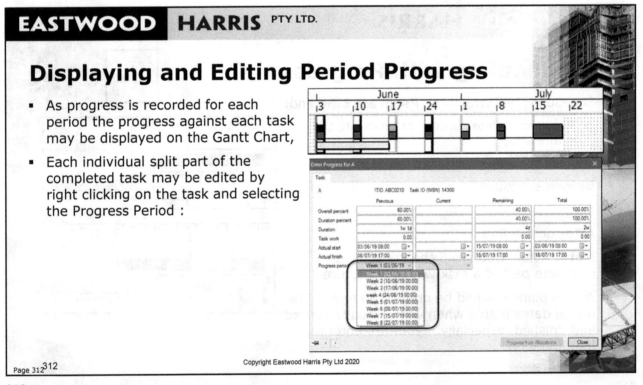

Page 312 312

312

---

15 - UPDATING AN UNRESOURCED PROJECT - SUMMARY

In this module we covered the following topics:

- Concepts for Updating an Unresourced Project
- Multiple Reports Dates
- Displaying Progress
- Progress Options and Setting the Progress Date
- Understanding the Percent Complete fields
- Entering Progress
- Overall Percent Complete Weighting
- Task Work
- Rescheduling with Progress.

Page 313 313   Copyright Eastwood Harris Pty Ltd 2020

313

Workshop 15 - Updating the Schedule and Baseline Comparison

- At the end of the first week you have to update the schedule and report progress and slippage.

Page 314 314   Copyright Eastwood Harris Pty Ltd 2020

314

EASTWOOD HARRIS PTY LTD.

16 - LIBRARY EXPLORER

- Project files contain many objects such as resources, codes, calendars, and currency units,

- These are stored in the Library Explorer,

- Objects may be simply copied from the Library Explorer in one project to a Library Explorer in another project.

315

EASTWOOD HARRIS PTY LTD.

Understanding Library Explorer

- To open **Library Explorer**:
  - Select the **View**, **Show**, **Library Explorer**, or
  - Select the **Library Explorer** button on the quick access tool bar:

24 object(s)	Contents of 'Project Objects'	
Project Objects	Resource Type	Total Number
Allocation Group	Allocation Group	1
Annotation Category	Annotation Category	4
Calendar	Calendar	18
Code Library	Code Library	8
Consumable Resource	Consumable Resource	12
Cost And Income Rate	Cost And Income Rate	27
Cost Centre	Cost Centre	17
Filter	Filter	29
Filter Category	Filter Category	7
Formula	Formula	20
Formula Category	Formula Category	5
Milestone Appearance	Milestone Appearance	27
Link Category	Link Category	8
Permanent Resource	Permanent Resource	35
Progress Period	Progress Period	11
	Quality Check	2

316

Library Explorer Tree and List View

- The **Library Explorer** has two panes:
  - The **Tree View** on the left displays the libraries,
  - The **List View** displays the objects in the library.

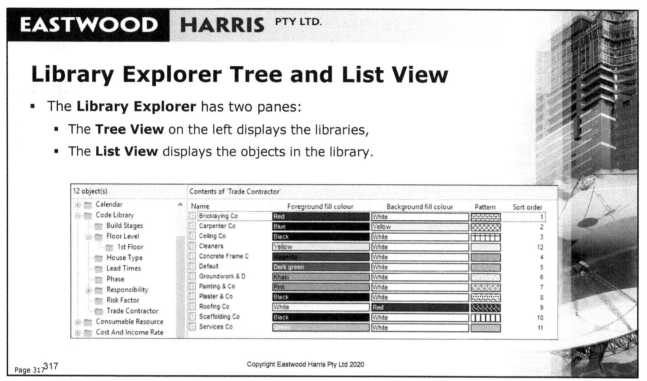

Copyright Eastwood Harris Pty Ltd 2020

317

Customising Library Explorer...

- All libraries are not displayed by default,
- To show or hide libraries right click a blank area of the **List View** then select **Show Libraries**:

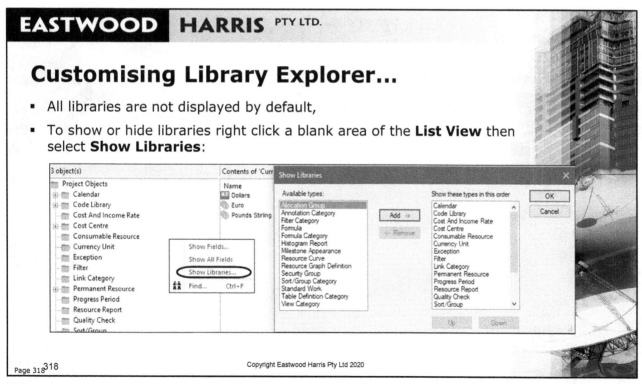

Copyright Eastwood Harris Pty Ltd 2020

318

Customising Library Explorer

- Select libraries in the **Library Explorer** from the right-hand list select **Remove** to remove a library,
- Select libraries in the **Library Explorer** from the right-hand list select **Add** to add a library,
- Use the **Up** and **Down** buttons to reorder the Libraries, an alphabetical order is useful:

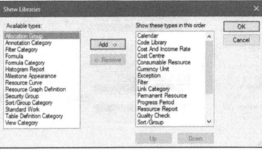

Workshop 16 – Library Explorer

- We will reformat the Library Explorer in this workshop.

158

EASTWOOD HARRIS PTY LTD.

17 - USER DEFINABLE FIELDS & WBS

- Powerproject allows the creation of **User Defined Fields** with formulae,
- For example you may want to add a specific comment field,
- These have a similar functionality to Microsoft Project Custom Fields in terms of the ability to assign formulae to calculate new data from other fields,
- Also they are similar to P6 User Definable fields but a lot more powerful.

321

EASTWOOD HARRIS PTY LTD.

Creating User Fields for your projects

- User **Field Manager** will not operate until the project has been saved,
- Select **Project**, **Properties**, **User Field Manager** command,
- Select **Add** to create a field,
- Select the type of field that you want to create and
- Assign a name for the field, it must not have spaces.

322

EASTWOOD HARRIS PTY LTD.

Work Breakdown Structure

- Work Breakdown Structure (WBS), a hierarchical structure which usually identifies the major deliverables,

- Like P6, the WBS may be created before activities are added and allows another method of organizing the activities,

- A well-structured WBS should:

  - Include all the project deliverables and

  - Be set at the appropriate level for summarizing project activities and reporting project progress,

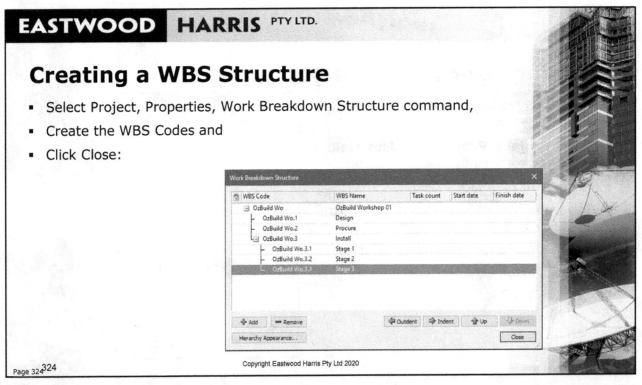

Copyright Eastwood Harris Pty Ltd 2020

Page 323

323

EASTWOOD HARRIS PTY LTD.

Creating a WBS Structure

- Select Project, Properties, Work Breakdown Structure command,

- Create the WBS Codes and

- Click Close:

WBS Code	WBS Name	Task count	Start date	Finish date
⊟ OzBuild Wo	OzBuild Workshop 01			
OzBuild Wo.1	Design			
OzBuild Wo.2	Procure			
⊟ OzBuild Wo.3	Install			
OzBuild Wo.3.1	Stage 1			
OzBuild Wo.3.2	Stage 2			
OzBuild Wo.3.3	Stage 3			

Copyright Eastwood Harris Pty Ltd 2020

Page 324

324

Assigning WBS Codes to Tasks

- The WBS Codes are assigned to tasks form **Project View** the in the same way as calendars and Codes,

- **NOTE:** To change the display of the WBS Hierarchy from **Code** to **Name**, select **File**, **Options**, **Views**,

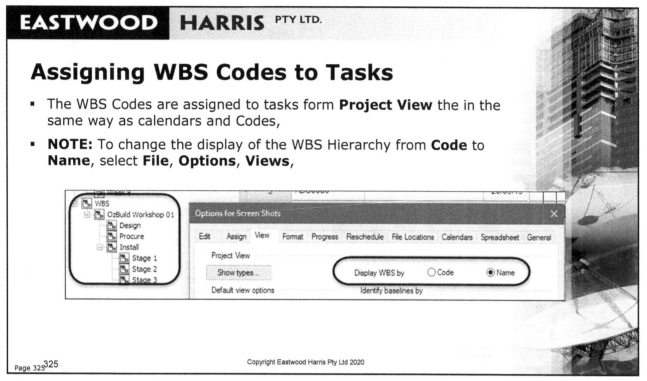

WBS Codes and Columns

- WBS Codes may be viewed and edited in the following columns
  - **WBS Code Identification,**
  - **WBS Name Identification:**

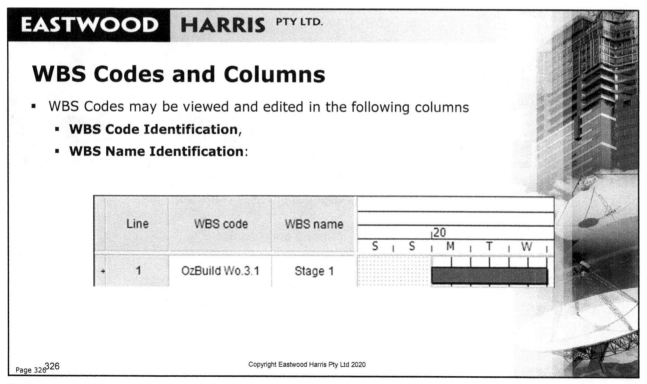

EASTWOOD HARRIS PTY LTD.

To Display by WBS

- To see the task grouped by WBS, you will need to:
- Set the **Hierarchy Appearance** from the **Work Breakdown** form, and
- Create or apply **a Sort and Group** by WBS:

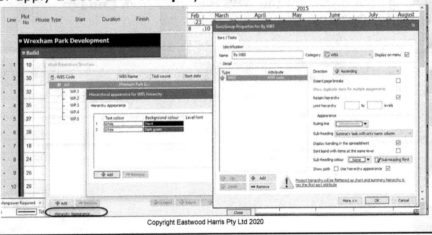

Page 327 327

327

EASTWOOD HARRIS PTY LTD.

Course Close

We have covered the following topics:

- Introduction to Powerproject and Creating a project
- Navigation and Setting Options
- Calendars
- Tasks and Milestones
- Summary Tasks
- Linking Tasks to create a Critical Path Schedule
- Constraints

- Other Task Types
- Formatting the Display
- Code Libraries
- Filters
- Organising Tasks using Sort and Groups
- Printing and Reports
- Baselines
- Updating an Unresourced Project
- User Definable Fields and WBS.

Page 328 328

328

EASTWOOD HARRIS PTY LTD.

Review Expectations

- Any questions,
- Complete Feedback Sheet,
- Have we met your expectations?

Page 329329   Copyright Eastwood Harris Pty Ltd 2020

329

EASTWOOD HARRIS PTY LTD.

Thank you for attending

Page 330330   Copyright Eastwood Harris Pty Ltd 2020

330

www.ingramcontent.com/pod-product-compliance
Lightning Source LLC
Chambersburg PA
CBHW060557060326
40690CB00017B/3739